Quilt a Gift
for Christmas

Quilt a Gift
for Christmas

21 beautiful projects to make with love

Barri Sue Gaudet

D&C
David and Charles

www.rucraft.co.uk

Contents

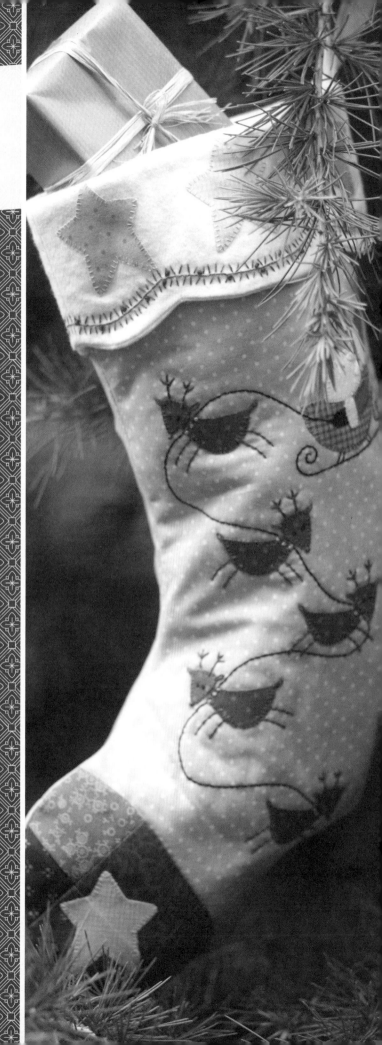

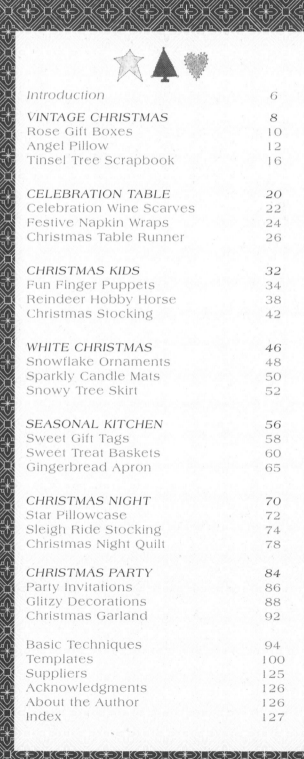

Introduction

Christmas is a wonderful time to give, join with
family and friends, celebrate, bake and make.
With this book to help you, you will be able
to fashion many lovely projects for all your
holiday events.

Created from your hand, we start with some
gorgeous projects to make on vintage holiday
themes, bringing us back to simpler times.
Following these are ideas for a well-laden
Christmas table and items for the seasonal
kitchen. Christmas is for children and there are
some fun projects for the excited little ones in
your life. There are beautiful decorations to
welcome all to your home and decorate the
house as a winter wonderland. There are also
ideas on celebrating a glistening party night, as
well as finally relaxing late on Christmas Eve
under a cozy quilt in front of the fire.

In each chapter of this book you will be
given a variety of designs for flexibility of
skill level and time available, so you can fit
a wonderful handmade gift into any holiday
occasion, whether you have just a few hours
free or a week. Hints and tips are included
to help you expand your capabilities with
new materials and techniques. Step-by-step

instructions on appliqué, embroidery, piecing and quilting are included to help you grow as a crafter and combine all these techniques into special creations.

I have designed the gifts, keepsakes and decorations in the book to suit every colour palette, with colours ranging from delicate whites, pinks, mints and aquas, to glittering golds and silvers, plus of course the traditionally bold reds and greens.

Your heart will brim with Christmas spirit as you progress through the book creating beautiful gifts and Christmas traditions. You may, like me, feel like one of Santa's elves as you make the magic of Christmas come alive through your handwork. I hope this book brings you lots of inspiration for this special time of year.

Barri Sue Gaudet

Vintage Christmas

Christmas is a time for tradition, for bringing out treasured family heirlooms and remembering good times past. This chapter celebrates those traditions with a selection of decorative projects adorned with fabric roses, ribbon leaf clusters and Christmas-themed embroidery motifs.

Charming hanging gift boxes in unusual angular cone shapes are decorated with plush roses and can be given as gifts or used to decorate the home each year. A cosy little pillow with an adorable embroidered angel is perfect in a little girl's room during the festive season. An attractive scrapbook featuring a tree festooned with tinsel and baubles will hold happy Christmas memories.

The colours in this chapter are a lovely mellow combination of cream, gold and antique rose, with touches of mint and caramel. Easy hand embroidery creates wonderful embellishment on the projects.

Rose Gift Boxes

A delightful cone-shaped box decorated with fabric roses and a sparkly pipe cleaner handle makes a gorgeous gift box. Why not make several, fill with goodies and hang them from the tree or mantel for Christmas morning?

You will need...
For one box

- Print fabric 12in (30.5cm) square
- Cardstock-weight paper, one 12in (30.5cm) square or two pieces 8½in x 11in (21.6cm x 28cm)
- Fusible web
- Freezer paper
- Rose-coloured wool felt for flowers 6in x 18in (15.2cm x 45.7cm)
- Mint ribbon ⅜in (1cm) wide x 2½yd (2.25m)
- One sparkly pipe cleaner
- Craft glue or hot glue gun and glue sticks
- Fabric glue or seam sealant liquid (optional)
- DMC stranded cotton (floss) in colour to match rose wool felt

Finished size:
8½in (21.6cm) tall x 3in (7.6cm) wide

›› Directions

1 To make the box, trace the outside border of the template (see the Template section) on to the paper side of fusible web. Press on to the wrong side of the fabric and cut out on the lines. Remove the paper so the glue side is exposed. Trace or copy pieces A, B, C, D, E, F, G and H on to cardstock paper. Cut out the eight separate pieces.

2 With the glue side of the fusible web (and wrong side of fabric) up, lay the cardstock pieces on to the fusible web following the design. If there is any overlap of paper, take the piece up and trim it. There should be a slight gap between each piece of paper for folding. Press the paper on to the fusible web.

3 Fold piece E to the inside and spread glue across from top to bottom. Place the opposite side (piece A) on top of E and press to hold. Make sure your bottom point is neat and covered with fabric. If any paper is showing trim it with scissors. Dab the bottom point with seam sealant (such as Fray Check) if desired. Set the box aside to dry.

4 Check the fit of the top flaps and trim if necessary. Bend top flap G towards the paper where it indents on each side. This should fit nicely to close.

5 To make the wool felt roses, trace one large and one small rose template on to the paper (dull) side of some freezer paper. Iron these traced pieces on to the rose wool felt and cut out on the traced line. Peel off the freezer paper.

6 Cut out one large rose shape and four small from wool felt. With two strands of matching embroidery cotton, starting at the larger end of the rose, work running stitch along the straight edge. Gather up the running stitch tightly and knot but do not cut the thread. Roll the rose into a pleasing spiral and use thread to anchor the spiral in place. Knot at the bottom and the back of the rose and cut the thread.

7 Cut one 20in (50cm) length of mint ribbon. Create figure-of-eight shapes with the ribbon, twice. The lengths should be approximately 3½in–4in (8.9cm–10.2cm). Use

sewing thread to anchor at the centre. Do the same for smaller roses but cut four 14in (35.5cm) lengths. The length of the figure-of-eighth should be about 2¼in (5.7cm). Anchor at the centre as before.

8 Position the roses on the box – the large rose on top of the box and four smaller roses on the sides about 1½in (3.8cm) down from the top on all sides. Glue on a ribbon cluster and then the wool felt rose on top (see photograph).

9 To attach the pipe cleaner handle, mark an X on the box pieces A and C. With a sharp instrument such as scissors, poke a tiny hole through the fabric and paper. Insert the pipe cleaner about ¼in (6mm) and bend it at 90 degrees. Put the other end into the opposite hole and bend. Finish by dabbing a bit of glue on the inside to hold the handle in place and allow to dry.

Angel Pillow

This gorgeous little pillow is so pretty with its embroidered angel and plump fabric roses.
Bring it out every year at Christmas time to tell everyone the festive season has arrived.

You will need...

- Tea-dyed or sand-coloured muslin ¼yd (0.25m)
- Mint green print fabric ⅛yd (12cm)
- Rose print fabric ⅛yd (12cm)
- Backing fabric ½yd (0.5m)
- Lightweight quilt wadding (batting) 16in x 18in (40.6cm x 45.7cm)
- Rose-coloured wool felt for flowers 6in x 18in (15.2cm x 45.7cm)
- Mint ribbon ⅜in (1cm) wide x 2¼yd (2m)
- Bag of toy stuffing
- Freezer paper
- Craft glue or hot glue gun and glue sticks
- DMC stranded cotton (floss): 420 tan, 3347 green, 310 black, white (blanc), 3721 red/rose, 3859 pink, 758 peach, 3820 yellow, 926 light blue, 921 orange, plus colour to match rose wool felt

Finished size:
12in x 15in (30.5cm x 38cm)

›› Directions

1 To make the centre for the embroidery cut a piece of muslin 8in x 10in (20.3cm x 25.4cm). Border this muslin with mint green fabric as follows. Cut two strips each 1½in x 10in (3.8cm x 25.4cm) and sew these to the top and bottom of the muslin using ¼in (6mm) seams. Press seams open. Cut two strips each 1½in x 12in (3.8cm x 30.5cm) and sew these to the sides of the muslin piece. Press seams open.

2　To make the rose borders, cut two strips each 2½in x 12in (6.4cm x 30.5cm) and sew these to the top and bottom. Press seams open. Cut two strips each 2½in x 14in (6.4cm x 35.5cm) and sew these to the sides. Press seams open.

3　See the Template section for the relevant templates. Trace the angel and scallop embroidery design on to the muslin centre. Back with quilt wadding (batting) before doing the embroidery, tacking (basting) the wadding in place.

4　Work the embroidery as described in the panel at the end of the project.

5　Cut a backing for the pillow 15in x 16in (38cm x 40.6cm). Pin the front and back pieces together, right sides facing. Sew all around, leaving an opening for turning through. Trim corners, turn right side out and stuff with toy stuffing. Slipstitch the opening closed.

6　To make the wool felt roses use the large rose template from the Rose Gift Box project. Trace one large rose on to the paper (dull) side of some freezer paper. Iron this traced piece on to the rose wool felt and cut out on the traced line. Peel off the freezer paper. Repeat for three more roses. With two strands of matching embroidery cotton, starting

at the larger end of the rose, work running stitch along the straight edge. Gather up the stitching tightly and knot but don't cut the thread. Roll the rose into a pleasing spiral and use thread to anchor it in place. Knot at the bottom and back of the rose and cut the thread.

7 Cut the mint ribbon into four 20in (50.8cm) lengths. Create figure-of-eight shapes with the ribbon, twice. The lengths should be about 3½in–4in (8.9cm–10.2cm). Use sewing thread to anchor at the centre of each.

8 Finish by gluing a ribbon leaf cluster on to each corner of the green border of the pillow and then a wool felt rose on top.

›› Embroidery

- Use three strands of embroidery cotton (floss) for white (blanc), one strand for black and two strands for all other colours. When all the embroidery is finished remove the tracing lines.
- Angel hair in tan backstitch. Cheeks on angel in pink backstitch. Eyes in black French knots. (1)
- Angel head, hands and feet in peach backstitch. Wings in white backstitch. Dress in light blue backstitch. Dots at neck edge in light blue French knots. All holly berries (three-dot clusters) on scallop and dress, and dots on halo in red/rose French knots. (2)
- All stars and flame in yellow backstitch, with the V shape inside the flame in orange straight stitch. Candle in white backstitch. Wick for candle in black straight stitch. (3)
- Asterisks on background in white straight stitch. Dots on background in white French knots. (4)
- All pine needles in green straight stitches. All scallop vine lines and halo in green backstitch. All leaves in green lazy daisy stitches. (5)

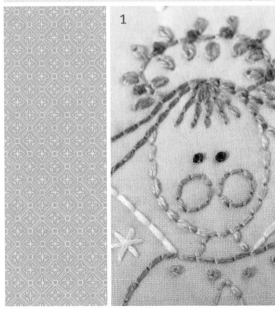

1

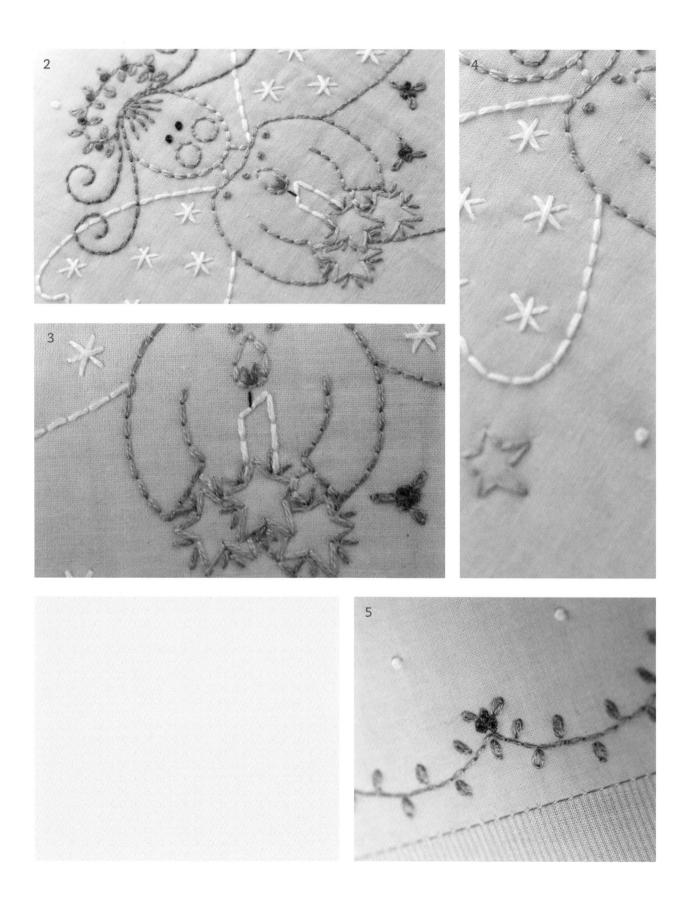

Tinsel Tree Scrapbook

A lovely Christmas tree design is perfect for decorating a scrapbook or photograph album cover – ideal to hold snapshots and memories of a wonderful family Christmas. The measurements for this project are based on the sizes given in the Tip below.

You will need...

- Tea-dyed or sand-coloured muslin ¼yd (0.25m)
- Mint green print fabric ⅛yd (12cm)
- Off-white fabric ¾yd (0.75m)
- Inside lining fabric ½yd (0.5m)
- Light quilt wadding (batting) one piece 9in x 10in (23cm x 25.4cm) and one 16in x 36in (40.6cm x 91.4cm)
- Rose-coloured wool felt for flowers 6in x 18in (15.2cm x 45.7cm)
- Mint ribbon ⅜in (1cm) wide x 2¼yd (2m)
- Freezer paper
- Fusible interfacing
- Craft glue
- Hot glue gun and glue sticks
- DMC stranded cotton (floss): 839 dark brown, 420 tan, 3347 green, 581 light green, 310 black, 646 grey, 3721 red/rose, 3859 pink, 3820 yellow, 832 gold, 931 blue, 926 light blue, 3041 lavender, 921 orange, white (blanc) and ecru, plus colour to match rose wool felt

Finished size:
13in x 15in (33cm x 38cm)

›› Directions

1 To make the embroidery centre, cut muslin 7½in x 8½in (19cm x 21.6cm). Border this with mint green fabric as follows. Cut two strips each 1½in x 8½in (3.8cm x 21.6cm) and sew to the sides of the muslin using ¼in (6mm) seams. Press seams open. Cut two strips each 1½in x 9½in (3.8cm x 24.1cm) and sew to the top and bottom of the muslin. Press seams open.

TIP

My album size is for scrapbook paper 12in (30.5cm) square, with metal rings inside for pages. The front and back are 13in (33cm) tall x 15in (38cm) wide. The spine is 2¾in x 13in (7cm x 33cm). If your scrapbook varies from this, alter the borders to fit.

2 Add off-white borders as follows (see Fig 1). Cut a piece 5in x 10½in (12.7cm x 26.7cm) for the right-hand border. Sew to the right side and press the seam open. Cut two pieces 3½in x 14in (8.9cm x 35.5cm) for the top and bottom. Sew to the top and bottom and press seams open. Cut a piece 16½in x 25in (42cm x 63.5cm) for the left-hand border. Sew to the left side and press the seam open. Check the fit to your album. The edges should extend to turn to the inside of album at least 1½in (3.8cm) on all sides.

3 See the Template section for the relevant templates. Trace the embroidery design on to the muslin centre and the scalloped holly on to the mint border. Back this area with wadding cut 9in x 10in (22.9cm x 25.4cm) and tacked (basted) in place. Work the embroidery as described in the panel at the end of the project.

4 Back the whole piece with quilt wadding cut 16in x 35in (40.6cm x 89cm). Tack (baste) in place.

5 Using a wash-away pen draw cross-hatch lines on to the off-white background ¾in (2cm) apart on a 45-degree angle. The lines should extend beyond the album edge to turn under. With two strands of pink embroidery thread, work running stitch lines through all layers. With three strands of rose/red work French knot dots at intersections of the cross-hatching on the front and spine area. With two strands of

green, work lazy daisy stitch leaves at every red/rose French knot, with the leaves in different directions. Remove tracing lines.

6 With thread matching the centre muslin, topstitch through all layers (two pieces of wadding) in the centre of the seam. Topstitch around the mint green border in the seam.

7 Lay the album open on top of the fabric piece. Trim, so at least 1in (2.5cm) extends all around the album. Allow for the bend in the spine in this measurement. With the fabric piece wrong side up, lay the album front on the fabric piece. Make sure the embroidery design is on the correct side and right side up when closed, and that it is centred on the front. Check that when the album closes and the spine is bent that the fit is still correct. With craft glue, glue the album front to the fabric wrong side, to hold while hot gluing. Starting with the corners, glue the corners to the inside of the cover on one side of the album. Now glue the corners on the opposite side. Hot glue at the spine to the inside. Continue gluing all edges to the inside, pulling taut and checking the fit often.

8 To make the inside lining, measure inside the cover front and back. Cut fusible interfacing to fit inside the front and back, up to the middle of the spine and ½in (1.3cm) from all outer edges. This should allow the inside lining to cover the raw edges of the top turned to the inside. If needed, cut two additional pieces of fusible interfacing to fit at the spine for a complete finished look. With an iron, press the interfacing to the wrong side of the lining fabric. Trim the lining fabric to match the fusible interfacing. Trim the outside corners to a slight curve if desired. Peel off the paper backing and press glue side down to the inside cover, front and back.

9 To make the roses, trace one large rose on to the paper side of some freezer paper. Iron this on to rose wool felt and cut out on the traced line. Peel off the paper. Repeat for three more roses. With two strands of embroidery thread, starting at the large end, work running stitch along the straight edge. Gather up the stitches tightly and knot, but don't cut the thread. Roll the rose into a spiral and use the thread to anchor it in place. Knot at the bottom and back and cut the thread.

Fig 1
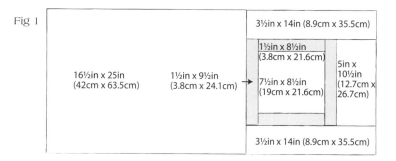

16½in x 25in (42cm x 63.5cm)   1½in x 9½in (3.8cm x 24.1cm)

3½in x 14in (8.9cm x 35.5cm)

1½in x 8½in (3.8cm x 21.6cm)

7½in x 8½in (19cm x 21.6cm)

5in x 10½in (12.7cm x 26.7cm)

3½in x 14in (8.9cm x 35.5cm)

10 Cut mint ribbon into four 20in (51cm) lengths, each about 4in (10.2cm). Create figure-of-eight shapes with the ribbon, twice. Use sewing thread to anchor at the centre where the ribbon crosses. Glue a ribbon leaf cluster on to the cover at each corner of the green border. Glue a rose on top.

» Embroidery

- Use three strands of embroidery cotton (floss) for white (blanc), one strand for black and two strands for all other colours. When all the embroidery is finished remove the tracing lines.
- Tan: tree trunk and bear muzzle in backstitch.
- Yellow: all stars and flames in backstitch. Ribbon on bottom present and vertical lines on present in backstitch, with lazy daisy stitch bow on top.
- Orange: all V shapes inside flames in straight stitch.
- Red/rose: all hearts, candy cane stripes, bottom present box shape, drum sides, left present vertical ribbon lines and chimney on dollhouse in backstitch. Bow on left present in lazy daisy stitch. All holly berries (three-dot clusters) on scallop in French knots.
- White: all candles and candy cane outlines in backstitch. Dots on right-hand present in French knots.
- Lavender: round ornaments on left side in backstitch.
- Gold: tree top star in backstitch and dots around star in French knots. Horn ornaments, drum circle top, drum bottom, stripes on round ornaments on left side in backstitch.
- Pink: bubble ornaments on top right branch and second to bottom left branch, right present box shape, stripe on round ornament second from the bottom right branch in backstitch. Stars on pink bubble ornaments in straight stitch. Dots on bottom of pink bubble ornaments in French knots.
- Blue: round ornament second branch from top right, sides of dollhouse in backstitch. Dots on drum in French knots.
- Light blue: bubble ornament second branch from bottom right, blanket under tree in backstitch. Bubble ornament star in straight stitch and dot on bottom of bubble in French knot.
- Light green: stripes on round ornament second from top right, round ornament second from bottom right, box shape on left present and vertical lines of ribbon on right present in backstitch. Bow on right present in lazy daisy stitch. Dots on bottom present in French knots.
- Grey: all round and bubble ornaments tops in backstitch.
- Dark brown: dollhouse roof and door, teddy bear head and body in backstitch. Teddy bear nose in satin stitch.
- Black: strings for all ornaments, wicks for candles, strings on drum, windows on dollhouse in backstitch. Teddy bear eyes in French knots.
- Green: all pine needles in straight stitches. All scallop vine lines on mint green border in backstitch. All leaves in lazy daisy stitches.
- Ecru: all garlands in French knot dots.

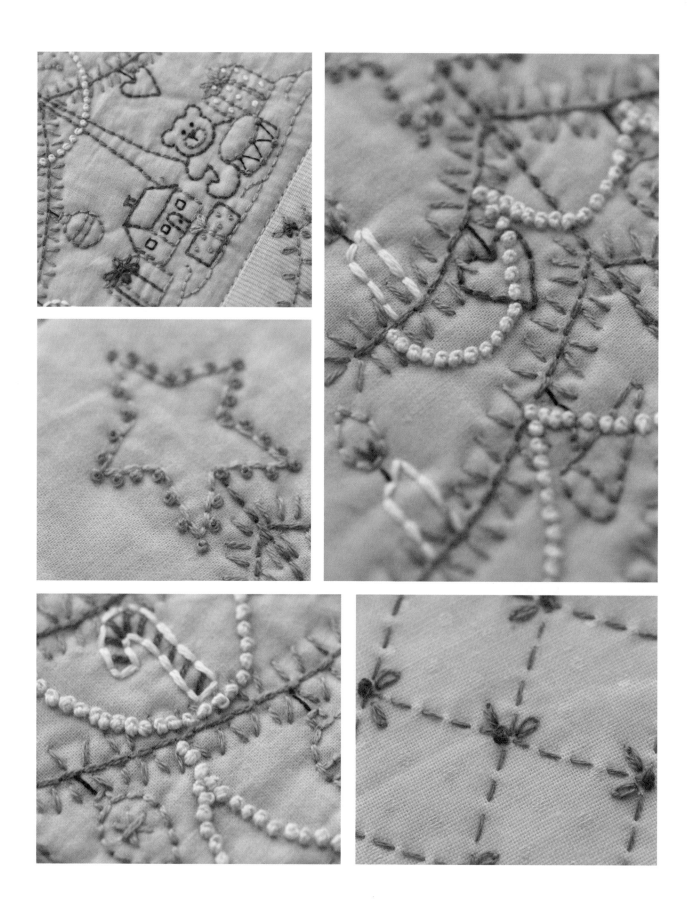

Celebration Table

Part of the joy of Christmas is feasting on all the wonderful foods prepared for the occasion. Making guests feel welcome at your table adds to the celebration.

Your spirits will be decked for the holiday table with some charming wine scarves. They are so fast it will be easy to accessorize wine bottles for the occasion. As you sit down to the Christmas table every guest will feel special with their own napkin holders. Each wrap can be customized with fun motifs to match your guests' personalities. A gorgeous table runner, with sweet images of Christmas that can be viewed from all sides of the table, makes a special project.

The colours chosen for this chapter are warm and welcoming ruby reds, bottle greens and dusky blues, with splashes of yellow and white for contrast. The bold stars and border embroidery add a delightful festive charm.

Celebration Wine Scarves

Give your table wines a festive collar with these cute scarves. They not only look good but prevent drips from staining your table runner. Four different designs have been supplied – a snowman, angel, Santa and stocking.

You will need...

For one scarf

- Blue wool felt 1½in x 18in (3.8cm x 44.7cm)

- Wool felt in red, light red, yellow, white, peach, brown and green, 3in (7.6cm) square of each

- Freezer paper

- Pinking shears

- DMC stranded cotton (floss): 433 brown, 3852 yellow, 355 red, 310 black, 976 orange, 3774 blush and blanc (white), plus colours to match wool felts

Finished size:
1¼in x 18in (3.2cm x 45.7cm)

>> Directions

1 Trim the edges of the strip of blue wool felt with pinking shears. See the Template section for the relevant templates. Trace the motifs for the ends of the scarf on to the paper side of the freezer paper. Press the shiny side to the correct colour of wool felt. Cut out on the lines. Peel the freezer paper off.

2 Glue or pin the appliqué motif to the ends of the scarf. Note that some pieces need to overlap. I did a star at one end and a heart on the other just above the motif. With a single strand of matching embroidery cotton, whipstitch the appliqués in place. Now work the embroidery as described in the panel to finish.

>> Embroidery

- Trace the embroidery lines with a wash-away marker or chalk pencil. Use two strands of embroidery cotton for all stitches.
- Stocking: work the dots in red French knots. (1)
- Santa: work the moustache with two white lazy daisy stitches and the eyes in black French knots. (2)
- Angel: backstitch the halo in yellow. Straight stitch the arms and legs in blush and eyes in black French knots. (3)
- Snowman: work the eyes, mouth and buttons in black French knots. Stitch the nose in orange satin stitch, the arms in brown backstitch and the scarf in red backstitch. (4)

>> TIP
To avoid stitches being seen on the back of the scarf, leave a 4in (10.2cm) strand of thread on the back when you bring up the thread to the front. Using a separate needle, thread this strand and make a tiny knot in the back and slip the needle through the wool felt a ½in (1.3cm) or so and then trim off excess thread.

 **2 day project**

Festive Napkin Wraps

Sweet napkin wraps will give your celebration table a coordinated look. There are four different designs – a snowman, angel, Santa and stocking – and you could make one of each or a set of the same design for the table.

You will need...

For one napkin wrap

- Blue wool felt 6in x 11in (15.2cm x 28cm)
- Dark blue wool felt 7in x 12in (17.8cm x 30.5cm)
- Red and white wool felt 4in (10.2cm) square of each
- Wool felt in green, yellow, light red, peach and brown, 3in (7.6cm) square of each
- Freezer paper
- Blue ribbon ⅝in (1.6cm) wide x 24in (61cm)
- DMC stranded cotton (floss): 580 green, 433 brown, 3852 yellow, 355 red, 310 black, 976 orange, 3768 blue, 3774 blush and blanc (white), plus colours to match wool felts

Finished size:
4½in x 10in (11.4cm x 25.4cm)

›› Directions

1 See the Template section for the relevant templates. Trace the napkin background (the solid line) on to the paper side of the freezer paper. Press the shiny side of the freezer paper on to the blue wool felt and cut out on the solid line. Cut out one for each napkin wrap.

> **›› TIP**
> *The freezer paper template can be re-used up to six times before losing its stickiness. Simply peel it off and press it on to a new piece of wool felt.*

2 Trace the heart shape on to freezer paper. Press on to red wool felt. Cut out one for each wrap. Trace two stars on to freezer paper and cut out two from yellow wool felt. Cut out two for each wrap. Trace your chosen motifs. Press on to the wool felt colours following the photographs, and then cut out all.

3 Glue or pin the motifs to the red hearts. Some appliqué pieces need to overlap. Using one strand of matching embroidery cotton, whipstitch the appliqué to the red heart. Now work the embroidery as described in the panel.

4 Glue or pin a red heart with motif and two stars to a blue background. Use a single strand of matching stranded cotton and whipstitch in place.

5 Glue or pin a finished blue background to a dark blue background, leaving the ends free for ribbon later. Whipstitch with a single strand of matching stranded cotton, leaving the ends free for ribbon.

6 Carefully trim the dark blue backing (the dashed line) ¼in–⅜in (6mm–10mm) from the edge of the blue background. With a tiny spot of glue or a pin, insert a 12in (30.5cm) length of ribbon in between the blue and dark blue at the ends. Finish the whipstitching where it was previously left free at the ends. Finish by using the ribbon to tie the wrap around the napkin.

>> Embroidery

- Trace the embroidery lines on to the appliqués and blue background with a removeable marker. Use three strands of embroidery cotton for all stitches.
- Snowman: work the eyes, mouth and buttons in black French knots. Work the scarf in blue backstitch and the nose in orange satin stitch. (1)
- Angel: work the halo in yellow backstitch, the arms and legs in blush straight stitches and the eyes in black French knots. (2)
- Santa: work the eyes in black French knots and the moustache in white lazy daisy stitches. (3)
- Stocking: work the stripes in blue backstitch and the dots in red French knots. (4)
- All: work the snow dots in blanc (white) French knots. Work the pine branch in brown backstitch, all berries in red French knots and all pine needles in green straight stitches. (5)

Christmas Table Runner

This is a lovely piece to bring out every year as the centrepiece of the Christmas table. The runner features five motifs, each contained within a red heart – an angel, stocking, Santa, snowman and house – repeated along both sides of the runner.

You will need...

- Blue wool felt 14in x 38in (35.5cm x 96.5cm) for background and a 6in (15.2cm) square for appliqué
- Dark blue wool felt for backing 16in x 40in (40.6cm x 101.6cm)
- Red wool felt for hearts 8in x 30in (20.3cm x 76.2cm)
- Yellow and white wool felt 9in (23cm) square of each
- Blush and tea-dyed or (sand-coloured) wool felt 3in (7.6cm) square of each
- Light red and brown wool felt 8in (20.3cm) square of each
- Freezer paper 13in x 48in (33cm x 122cm)
- DMC stranded embroidery cotton (floss): 580 green, 433 brown, 3852 yellow, 3768 blue, 310 black, 976 orange, 3774 blush, 355 red and blanc (white), plus colours to match wool felts

Finished size:
12¼in x 34in (31cm x 86.4cm)

>> **TIP**

To trace embroidery designs on to wool felt use a black felt-tip pen and trace the designs on to tulle fabric first (which is a netting, like a bridal veil). Place the tulle over the wool felt shape and using a wash-away marker carefully go over the black pen markings. Most of the wash-away pen will go through the holes and on to the felt. Fill in where necessary.

>> Directions

1 See the Template section for the relevant templates. The runner is shown in two parts. See the photograph below for the layout. Trace the solid line for the background on to the paper side of the freezer paper. The centre of the runner is marked with a cross, while dotted lines indicate where the middle length and width is. Note where the middle point is and radiate out from this point on four sides. Press the shiny side of the freezer paper on to the blue felt and cut one background. Set aside for now.

2 Trace one or two large hearts on to the paper side of the freezer paper. Cut out twelve hearts. Trace one or two stars on to freezer paper. Cut out eleven stars. Trace one each of the motifs on to freezer paper. There are six snow pieces on the hearts. Cut six from white wool felt for the snowmen and the houses.
Snowmen: cut three snowmen from white wool felt and three blue scarves.
Houses: cut three blue houses, three brown roofs and doors, six sand windows and six green trees.
Angels: cut two blue dresses, two white wings, two blush faces and two yellow halos.

Santa: cut two brown reindeer bodies and heads, two light red saddles, two light red coats and hats, four white cuffs, two white beards, two trims and two hat balls, two blush faces and four black mittens.
Stocking: cut two green stockings, two brown toes and two white cuffs.

3 Pin or glue the motifs on to the hearts. With one strand of matching embroidery cotton, whipstitch them in place. Note that some pieces overlap, as indicated by the dashed lines on the templates. For the moment it will be necessary to leave the Santa appliqué partly unstitched where he comes off the heart. Now work the embroidery as described in the panel.

>> Embroidery

- Trace embroidery lines for the heart motifs on to the appliqués with a removeable marker. Use three strands of embroidery cotton throughout.
- House: stitch the tree trunks in brown straight stitches, outline the windows and panes with brown straight stitches. Work the door knob in a black French knot. (1)
- Snowman: work the eyes, mouth and buttons in black French knots, the nose in orange satin stitch and the arms in brown backstitch. (2)
- Angel: work the eyes in black French knots, the arms and legs in blush backstitch, the holly swag in green backstitch, the berries in red French knots and the pine needles in green straight stitch. (3)
- Santa and reindeer: work Santa's eyes and buttons and the reindeer eyes in black French knots. Work Santa's moustache in two white lazy daisy stitches and the reindeer ears and tail in brown lazy daisy stitches. Work the reindeer legs and antlers in brown backstitch, the collar in red backstitch and the bells on the collar in yellow French knots. Note: the reindeer hind legs will need to be embroidered later when the heart is placed on the background. (4)
- Stocking: work the stripes in blue backstitch and the dots as red French knots. Work the snow dots on the hearts in white French knots. (5)

4 Pin or glue the hearts and stars in place on the blue background. With one strand of matching embroidery cotton, whipstitch these in place. With one strand finish whipstitching Santa in place on the blue background. With three strands of brown, finish backstitching the reindeer legs on the blue background.

5 Mark the embroidery lines for the pine bough around the edge of the runner and also the dots and pine needles on the stars. Using three strands of embroidery cotton, work the pine bough line in brown backstitch, the berries in red French knots and all pine needles in green straight stitches.

6 Pin or glue the finished runner on to the dark blue wool felt backing. With one strand of blue embroidery cotton whipstitch it to the backing. To finish, carefully trim the dark blue backing ¼ in–⅜in (6mm–10mm) from the lighter blue edge.

Christmas Kids

Most adults love Christmas but few would doubt that it is really a time for children. The hours spent choosing presents are worth it just to see their excitement as they rip off the wrappings and begin to play. The projects in this chapter are sure to keep the children in your life happy.

There is a range of cute finger puppets that will provide hours of pleasure for young children and be the focus of many story-time games. Older kids will love the reindeer hobby horse, with his cuddly head, fun antlers and polka dot reins. And finally, what Christmas is complete without a stocking, especially one filled with little gifts? This one is made from strip-pieced fabrics adorned with beloved Christmas figures, including Santa, reindeer, elf and snowman.

The colours in this chapter are bright and cheerful, with plenty of fun reds, greens, blues and yellows to appeal to children.

Fun Finger Puppets

Children will love these sweet finger puppets, which are really easy to make. There are five delightful designs to play with – a Santa, reindeer, elf, snowman and angel.

You will need...

For five puppets

- Wool felt 10in (25.4cm) square of each in red, white, light green, brown and blue

- Wool felt 5in (12.7cm) square of each in yellow, green, orange, pink, peach, oatmeal, dark brown and black

- Freezer paper

- Glue or pins

- DMC stranded cotton (floss): 310 black and colours to match wool felt colours – for the blanket stitch I used: blanc (white), 433 dark brown, 469 dark green, 470 light green, 931 blue, 3774 peach and 3777 red

Finished size:
3½in x 1½in (8.9cm x 3.8cm)

>> Directions

1 See the Template section for the relevant templates. Trace the shapes for the finger puppets on to the paper side of the freezer paper. If you have a hole punch, use it to cut out the balls for the Santa and elf hats. I also used it for the pink cheeks on the elf and angel and the reindeer nose. Trace the finger puppet sleeve shapes on to the paper side of the freezer paper.

2 Press the freezer paper shapes on to the correct colours of wool felt. Now follow the individual instructions for each puppet.

3 For the snowman: cut two snowman shapes from white wool felt. Cut two arms from brown. Cut one nose from orange. The scarf is one strip of blue wool felt cut almost ¼in (6mm) wide x 3in (7.6cm) long.

>> TIP

It is much easier to use small dabs of glue to hold these little appliqué pieces together than pins. Just place a dot of glue where needed, pinch with your fingers and allow to dry for a bit before proceeding.

4 Glue (or pin) the nose in place and whipstitch with a single strand of matching stranded cotton. Wrap the scarf in place around the head and whipstitch in place. With three strands of black stranded cotton, stitch French knots for the eyes, mouth and buttons.

5 Sew the back of the snowman to one side of the sleeve. The bottom of the snowman should be just above the straight edge of the sleeve and the head should project past the fold of the sleeve. Sew down the middle (the dotted line on the sleeve) through both layers from the fold to the bottom approximately 1¾in (4.4cm).

6 Glue (or pin) the arms in place. Glue the snowman front to match the snowman back, with the arms sandwiched between. With two strands of white, blanket stitch the snowman layers together.

7 To make up, fold the sleeve at the fold line wrong sides together. Starting at the top (fold), blanket stitch the top, sleeve side and through the front layer of the sleeve bottom and up other side.

8 For the reindeer: cut one back, one head, one body, two arms, and two ears from brown wool felt. Cut two antlers from oatmeal wool felt. Cut one nose and two hooves from dark brown wool felt.

9 Glue (or pin) the nose to the head. Glue the head to the body. Glue the hooves to the arms. With one strand of dark brown stranded cotton, whipstitch in place. Use three strands of black for French knot eyes.

10 Sew the back of the reindeer to one side of the sleeve. The bottom of the reindeer should be just above the straight edge of the sleeve. Sew down the middle (the dotted line on the sleeve) through both layers from the fold to the bottom of the reindeer back approximately 1¾in (4.4cm).

matching stranded cotton (head brown and dress blue) blanket stitch the layers together. Finish around the face with two strands of peach. To make up, follow step 7 for the snowman.

11 Glue the arms, antlers and ears in place. Glue the front to the back with arms, ears and antlers sandwiched between. With two strands of brown stranded cotton blanket stitch the layers together around the head and body. To make up, follow step 7 for the snowman.

12 For the angel: cut two dresses from blue wool felt. Cut one head from brown and one from peach. Cut one hair from brown. Cut one wing from white and halo from yellow. Cut two cheeks from pink.

13 Glue the hair and cheeks to the peach head. With one strand of matching stranded cotton, whipstitch the hair and cheeks in place. Glue one dress piece to the peach head. Use three strands of black to stitch French knot eyes.

14 Glue one dress and brown head to one side of the sleeve matching the angel front. The head and dress will overlap. The bottom of the dress should be just above the straight edge of the sleeve. The head will stick up past the sleeve fold line. Sew down the middle (dotted line) through both layers.

15 Glue the wings in place. Glue the front to the back with wings sandwiched between. Glue the halo on the back of the head. With two strands of

16 For the elf: cut two elf bodies and two hats from light green wool felt. Cut two heads from peach. Cut two cheeks from pink. Cut two hat trims, two hat balls and one belt from dark green. Cut one belt buckle from yellow.

17 Glue the cheeks to one head and the belt and buckle to one body. With one strand of matching stranded cotton, whipstitch in place. Glue two hat pieces together. With two strands of light green, blanket stitch together. Place one hat ball on to the top. Back with the other hat ball (with the hat sandwiched between) and blanket stitch in place with two strands of dark green. Glue the elf front together, the head to the body and one hat trim to hold the head to the hat. Use three strands of black to stitch French knot eyes.

18 Glue one body to one head, matching the front. The body and head will overlap as in the front. Glue to one side of the sleeve with the bottom of the body just above the straight edge of the sleeve. The head will project up past the sleeve fold line. Sew down

blanket stitch together. Place one hat ball on to the top. Back with the other hat ball (with the hat sandwiched between). With two strands of white, blanket stitch the hat balls together. Glue the front together, the beard to the body and the hat trim, which holds the hat to the face/beard. Use three strands of black for French knot eyes.

22 Glue or pin the remaining Santa body to the white head, matching the size of the front. Pieces will overlap as in the front. Glue or pin to one side of the sleeve with the body just above the straight edge of the sleeve. The head will stick up past the fold line of the sleeve. Sew down the middle (the dotted line) through the layers approximately 1¾in (4.4cm).

23 Glue the front to the back. Glue the remaining hat trim piece to the back, matching the front. With two strands of matching stranded cotton, blanket stitch the layers together, using red for the body and white around the beard, hat trim, moustache and face. To make up follow step 7 for the snowman.

the middle (the dotted line) through both layers approximately 1¾in (4.4cm).

19 Glue the front to the back. Glue the remaining hat trim to the back of the head, matching the front. With two strands of matching stranded cotton, blanket stitch the layers together, using light green for the body, dark green for hat trim and peach for the head. To make up follow step 7 for the snowman.

20 For the Santa: cut two bodies and two hats from red wool felt. Cut one beard, two hat trims, two moustache pieces and two hat balls from white. Cut one face from peach. Cut one belt from black and one belt buckle from yellow.

21 Glue the belt and buckle to one body piece. With one strand of matching stranded cotton, whipstitch in place. Glue the face to the beard and the moustache to the face/beard piece. Glue this face/beard piece to the body with the belt. Glue two hats together. With two strands of matching stranded cotton (red)

2 day project

Reindeer Hobby Horse

Hobby horses have been played with for centuries and this sweet reindeer version is bound to be much loved and used at Christmas and the rest of the year too.

You will need...

- Brown fleece ⅝yd (0.6m) of 54in (137cm) wide
- Tan wool felt for ears 8in (20.3cm) square
- Black wool felt for nose 3in (7.6cm) square
- Green wool felt for holly 4in (10.2cm) square
- Black fabric for eyes 6in (15.2cm) square
- Two self-cover buttons for eyes ⅞in (2.2cm) diameter
- Freezer paper
- Large bag of stuffing 1lb (450g)
- Four pipe cleaners
- Glue
- Long tweezers
- Ribbon ½in (1.3cm) wide x 3yd (2¾m)
- Buttons: two brown 1in (2.5cm) and two red ½in (1.3cm)
- Bells: four gold and two red each 1in (2.5cm)
- Wood dowel 1in (2.5cm) diameter x 28in (71cm) (or old broomstick) sanded well
- DMC stranded cotton (floss): 433 brown, 310 black and 3777 red

Finished size of reindeer head:
18in (45.7cm) tall x 12in (30.5cm) wide

» Directions

1 Sewing seams are ⅜in (1cm) for all of the reindeer's head and ears and ⅛in (3mm) for the antlers. See the Template section for the relevant templates. Begin by tracing on the solid line one each of the reindeer head/neck, back of head/neck, ear, nose and antler shapes on to freezer paper. The solid line is the cutting line and the dashed lines are sewing lines.

2 With the brown fleece doubled, wrong sides together, press the freezer paper shapes on to the fleece. Use pins to hold the paper temporarily while you cut the shapes. Cut two head/necks, two back of head/necks, two ears and four antlers. Cut one nose from black wool felt and two ears from tan felt.

3 With right sides together on the head/neck piece sew the dart at the nose on both head/neck shapes. Use your sewing machine's reverse stitch to anchor well.

4 With right sides together, pin the head/neck pieces and sew the centre front seam from top of the head to bottom of the neck. With right sides together, sew the centre back seam of the back of the head/neck pieces.

5 With right sides together, sew a fleece ear to a tan felt ear, leaving open at the bottom. Turn right side out. With brown stranded cotton, turn the sides of the ear bottoms to the centre of the ear bottom and hand stitch in place. Repeat for the other ear. Pin the ears right sides to the head/neck front (in between the Xs marked on the template) with tan wool felt to the right side of the fleece.

6 With right sides together, sew the antlers with a ⅛in (3mm) seam. Leave open where shown for turning.

Clip the inside of the curves. Turn the antlers right side out and then whipstitch the opening closed. Take small bits of stuffing and stuff into each 'finger' of antler so there is at least ½in (1.3cm) of stuffing in each. Bend the top of two pipe cleaners over by ½in (1.3cm). Stick the bent end of the pipe cleaner into the centre finger of both of the three-fingered antlers. Finish stuffing the antler until it is stiff. Leave ¾in (2cm) free of stuffing at the bottom. Repeat for the other antler.

7 With right sides together, pin the antlers at the circle marked on the head/neck piece. My antlers were pinned so the three fingers were pointing out from the centre seam. With right sides together and matching centre seams, pin the head/neck to the back of head/neck, making sure the antlers and ears are inside. Start at the centre seam and sew from the top centre to the bottom. Repeat for the other side.

8 To make the eyes, use the self-cover buttons and follow the manufacturer's instructions to cover with black fabric. Using a scrap of fleece, sew on the buttons, with the fleece on the wrong side for extra strength. Sew well with six strands of black stranded cotton.

9 Stuff the head well with stuffing just to the jaw. I used a rubber band to hold the stuffing inside for the next steps. Pin the nose in place and whipstitch with three strands of black stranded cotton.

10 Cut two ribbons each 8in (20.3cm) long. Pin the ribbons in place for the bridle around the mouth. With one strand of red stranded cotton, whipstitch the ribbon. Trim the ends where they meet. Cut one ribbon for the bridle and reins 2¼ yd (2m) long. Mark the centre of the ribbon at 40½ in (103cm). Pin the centre of the ribbon to the centre back seam where shown. Using pins, bring both sides of the ribbon around the reindeer head to the ribbon around the mouth. Where the ribbon meets, fold the ribbon for the reins so it points back and then anchor with a pin. Leave the reins free for now. Whipstitch the ribbon in place around the head with red stranded cotton. Stack a red button on top of a brown button and with six strands of red sew in place where all the ribbons meet.

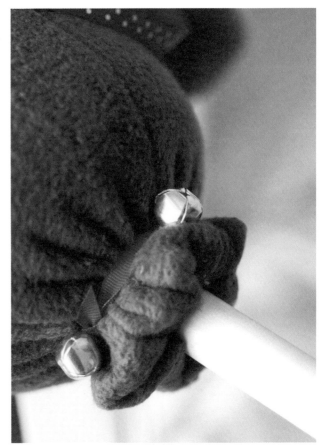

11 Cut two holly leaves from green wool felt. Sew two red bells to the holly ends. Sew in place at an antler with six strands of red.

12 Remove the rubber band and trim the neck edges even. Turn up the neck edges to the inside by 1½in (3.8cm). Working with six strands of brown and starting with a 9in (22.9cm) tail, work running stitch around the neck edge 1¼in (3.2cm) from the turned edge. Leave a 9in (22.9cm) tail at the end.

13 Stick the length of dowel into the reindeer head as far as it will go and stuff well all around the dowel to hold it in the middle of the reindeer neck. When you cannot stuff anymore, tighten the thread and squeeze glue into the neck for extra hold. Secure and tie off the thread. Set the reindeer aside until the glue dries.

14 Cut a 12in (30.5cm) length of ribbon. Sew three bells to the ribbon, spaced from the centre about 1¼in (3.2cm) apart. Place glue on the strip around the neck edge where knotted. Tie the ribbon to the reindeer neck on top of the glue and trim the ends. Sew the last bell on top of the knot and allow to dry. Tie the reins together at a comfortable distance, tie into a bow and then trim the ends to finish.

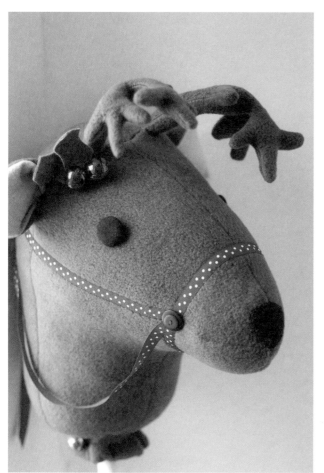

 1 week project

Christmas Stocking

A Christmas stocking is a must for any child (and some grown-ups too!) and this one will be great fun to fill with gifts. If bells are to be used this stocking is recommended for children over four years old. For safety, omit the bells for younger children.

You will need...

- Three blue fabrics for stocking front and back ¼yd (0.25m) of each

- Off-white fabric for cuff, hanger and lining ⅝yd (0.6m)

- Two green wool felts for trees, bows and elf belt and trims 8in (20.3cm) square each

- Brown wool felt for reindeer, tree trunks and snowman arms 7in (17.8cm) square

- Red wool felt for Santa and presents 6in (15.2cm) square

- White wool felt for Santa and snowman 6in (15.2cm) square

- Wool felts in dark brown, black, light green, yellow, peach, pink, orange, blue and oatmeal 4in (10.2cm) square each

- Freezer paper

- Wadding (batting) 20in (50.8cm) square

- Five gold bells 1in (2.5cm)

- DMC stranded cotton (floss): 310 black, 469 green, 931 blue, 3777 red, 3821 yellow, blanc (white), plus colours to match wool felts

Finished size:
19in x 13in (48.3cm x 33cm)

» Directions

1 See the Template section for the relevant templates. Trace the stocking top, heel and toe piece on to freezer paper. Note: the solid line is the sewing line and the dotted line is the cutting line.

2 Cut two heel pieces from a doubled piece of one of the blue fabrics. (There will be a duplicate heel for the back of the stocking.)

3 Use fabric strips to create the top and heel portion of the stocking as follows. Cut strips 1¾in x 9in (4.4cm x 22.9cm) from the three colours of blue fabric. Sew seven together along the 9in (22.9cm) length for the toe portion and nine together for the top portion. Do this step twice for the front and the back.

4 With the fabric strips created, place them wrong sides together and press the freezer paper template on to the corresponding strips (seven strips for the toe, nine strips for the top). Cut two of each. Sew the sections together for two stockings front and back. Set the back aside for now.

5 Trace the embroidery and appliqué lines on to the front of the stocking (the one with the toe pointing to the left). Tack (baste) the wadding (batting) to this stocking piece. You could tack with thread, use pins or spray baste.

6 Trace the appliqué pieces on to the paper side of the freezer paper. Thick lines are appliqué and thin lines are embroidery. A dashed line indicates where appliqué pieces overlap. After tracing and cutting out each appliqué shape, press these on to the corresponding wool felt colours. Cut out the appliqués and glue or pin in place. The snowman scarf is one strip of wool felt 4in (10.2cm) wide. Wrap the scarf around the back of the snowman head and cross in the front. With a single strand of matching embroidery cotton, whipstitch the appliqués in place on the stocking front. Work the embroidery as described in the following panel.

> ### » TIP
> *Use a hole punch to cut wool felts for the berries on the cuff, the hat balls on the Santa and elf hats and the reindeer noses.*

>> Embroidery

- All embroidery is worked with three strands of embroidery cotton. The cuff embroidery is worked later.
- Work all eyes in black French knots. Work Santa's buttons and the snowman mouth and buttons in black French knots. (1)
- Work the elf's buttons in green French knots and the dots on the presents in white French knots. (2)
- Work the reindeer collars in red backstitch with yellow French knot bells. Work the stars on the trees in white straight stitches. (3)
- Work the background swirls in white running stitches. (4)

7 Create a freezer paper stocking shape. Press the freezer paper on to the doubled white fabric with wrong sides together. Cut two and set these aside. Trace the cuff on to the paper side of the freezer paper on the dashed line. Press and cut four cuffs from white fabric doubled wrong side together.

8 Trace the embroidery lines of the swirls and appliqué placements on to one of the cuff pieces. Back the cuff traced with wadding (batting). Trace a few holly leaves on to the paper side of the freezer paper and press on to the two green wool felts. Cut twelve leaves from green felts and seven berries from red felt. Glue or pin in place and whipstitch down with one strand of matching stranded cotton. With three strands of blue work running stitch swirls on the cuff.

9 Place the cuff pieces right sides together, sew the cuff stitched and backed with wadding to the blank cuff together at the sides. Repeat for the remaining two. Press seams open. Place one cuff set into the other cuff set, right sides together, matching seams. Sew along the bottom, turn right side out and press well, with raw edges matching along the top.

10 With right sides together, sew the stocking front to the matching stocking back all around, leaving the top open. Turn right side out and press.

11 With right sides together, sew the white stocking linings with a slightly larger seam than the pieced stockings (⅜in/1cm). Leave a 5in (12.7cm) opening in the stocking lining. Start 1in (2.5cm) above the heel, leave 5in (12.7cm) open and then continue sewing to the top of the stocking. Do not turn right side out.

12 To make the tab hanger, cut a piece of white fabric 2in x 7½in (5cm x 19cm). Turn under ¼in (6mm) on both long edges to the wrong side and press. Fold in half again, wrong sides together. Topstitch along both long edges, leaving the ends undone.

13 Pin the cuff to the top of the stocking front, with the stitched front matching the front of the stocking and matching the seams. Fold the hanger in half and pin at the right seam (the heel side). Tack (baste) through all layers all around the top.

14 Put the outside stocking inside the white lining stocking (right sides together). Match seams and pin around the top. Sew all around twice for strength. Reach into the opening left in the stocking lining and pull everything right side out. Push the stocking lining to the inside of the front stocking. Press along the top. Finish your stocking by sewing the five gold bells (if using) to the front of the stocking cuff.

White Christmas

*Let it snow, let it snow, let it snow...
Those of us living in northern climes all
long for snow at Christmas – the soft,
white covering that brings a peaceful
atmosphere to this time of year.*

*Plump, round ornaments decorated with
white snowflake appliqués are perfect
to decorate the tree. You can also bring
a lovely atmosphere to your home
with some easy to make candle mats,
which use sparkle felt for the snowflake
appliqués. A beautiful tree skirt is a
fabulous project to create and is sure
to be used with pleasure every year.
Different snowflake shapes are created
in appliqué and scattered all over.*

*The colours used in this chapter reflect
our wishes for a white Christmas – pure
whites, the palest of blues and some
frost-glittered felt. Semi-transparent
gauze ribbon and delicate little seed
beads add to the ethereal look.*

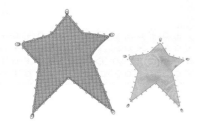 **3-4 hour project**

Snowflake Ornaments

A wintry scene will hang from the tree with these easy ornaments. Make several and watch the snowflakes sparkle and the white chiffon ribbon bows shine through the branches. Three different designs are provided.

You will need...

For one ornament

- Light blue fabric ½yd (0.3m) for background and lining
- White sparkle felt for snow-flake appliqués 9in (23cm) square
- Freezer paper
- White beads 8mm diameter
- Ribbon for hanger and bow 1in (2.5cm) wide x 1yd (1m)
- Polystyrene (Styrofoam) ball 3in (7.6cm) diameter
- Craft glue
- DMC stranded cotton (floss) in blanc (white) and to match light blue fabric

Finished size:
3in (7.6cm) diameter x 4in (10.2cm) tall

❯❯ Directions

1 See the Template section for the relevant templates. One quarter of each design is supplied. Draw an 11in (27.9cm) diameter circle for the background and lining on to the paper side of the freezer paper by copying the template and then turning the freezer paper to create the other quadrants to make a complete circle. Press the shiny side on to the light blue fabric. Cut out two circles from fabric. Peel the freezer paper off. One piece will be the front and one will be the lining.

2 Trace the snowflakes on to the paper side of the freezer paper. Press the shiny side of the freezer paper to the wrong side of the sparkle wool felt. Cut out the snowflakes. There are three, four or six snowflakes on the ornament depending on the design chosen.

3 Glue or pin the snowflakes to the light blue front piece, where shown on the template. With one strand of blanc (white) stranded cotton, whipstitch the snowflakes in place and then sew the beads to the middles and points of the snowflakes.

5 With right sides together, sew the lining to the front piece all around the circle. Carefully pull the lining from the front and use scissors to cut a slit in the centre of the lining about 3in (7.6cm) long. Pull it right side out through the slit and then press.

6 With a 24in (61cm) length of blue stranded cotton (six strands), sew a running stitch about 1in (2.5cm) from the edge all around. Place the foam ball inside, with the ribbon hanger facing up and out. Pull up the running stitches to gather the fabric around the ball. Tie a knot and trim cotton ends to ½in (1.3cm). Adjust the gathers into a pleasing look and tie the ribbon bow to finish.

4 Prepare the foam ball, making a hole in it for the ribbon hanger with a stick or pencil. Fill the hole with glue. Fold a 10in (25.4cm) length of ribbon in half, poke the ribbon ends into the hole and let the glue dry.

 2 day project

Sparkly Candle Mats

It may be cold outside, but the warm glow of candles atop these mats will set the scene for a wonderful white Christmas indoors. They are very easy to make from light blue wool felt, shimmering white felt and glittering glass beads. Three sizes are described.

You will need...

You will need...

- Light blue wool felt for background: 8in (20.3cm) square for small size, 9in (22.9cm) for medium and 14in (35.5cm) for large

- White sparkle felt for backing: 9in (22.9cm) square for small size, 10in (25.4cm) square for medium and 15in (38cm) square for large

- White sparkle felt for snowflake appliqués 9in (22.9cm) square

- Freezer paper

- White beads 8mm diameter and 10mm diameter

- DMC stranded cotton (floss) in blanc (white) and a blue to match the light blue wool felt

Finished size:
Small: 8½in (21.6cm) diameter
Medium: 9½in (24.1cm) diameter
Large: 14½in (36.8cm) diameter

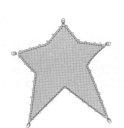

>> Directions

1 See the Template section for the relevant templates. One half of the small design and one half of the medium design is supplied. The full design is supplied for the large mat. For the small and medium designs, trace the scallop circle for the background on to the paper side of the freezer paper and then turn the freezer paper to copy the other side, making a complete scalloped circle. Iron the shiny side of the freezer paper on to the light blue wool felt. Peel the paper off. Prepare the large mat by using the full template and the same freezer paper method.

2 Trace the snowflakes on to the paper side of the freezer paper and then press the shiny side of the freezer paper to the wrong side of the sparkle wool felt. Cut out the snowflakes. There are four each of two different snowflakes on each mat.

3 Glue or pin the snowflakes to the light blue background where shown on the template. With one strand of blanc (white) stranded cotton, whipstitch the snowflakes in place. Dashed lines indicate where pieces join.

4 With one strand of blanc (white) stranded cotton, sew the beads to the middles, points and circle ends of the snowflakes. I used small beads on the small mat and large beads on the medium and large mats. With one strand of white, sew beads scattered about on the light blue background of the mat.

5 Leaving a ½in (1.3cm) edge on all sides, glue or pin the finished light blue background to the white sparkle felt backing. With one strand of light blue, whipstitch the background to the backing. Trim the backing ¼in (6mm) from the edge of the light blue background to finish.

Snowy Tree Skirt

Snowflakes shimmer and shine on this elegant Christmas tree skirt. The lights from the tree will glow in the little beads added to the snowflakes. A tulle ruffle at the base of the skirt adds to the image of a white Christmas.

You will need...

- Light blue fabric for front and back of tree skirt 3½yd (3.25m)
- White sparkle felt for snow-flakes ¾yd (0.75m)
- White beads 8mm diameter
- White wired ribbon for ties 1½in (3.8cm) wide x 2yd (2m)
- Tulle or netting for ruffled edge 1yd (1m) of 54in (137.2cm) wide
- Freezer paper
- Light quilt wadding (batting) 55in (140cm) square
- DMC stranded cotton (floss) in blanc (white)

Finished size:
50in (127cm) diameter

>> Directions

1 See the Template section at the back of the book for the relevant templates. One sixth of the design is supplied. Trace the skirt template on to freezer paper or template plastic and cut out on the solid line. The dashed line is the sewing line (¼ in/6mm seam). The dotted line is the centre of the template. Press or trace the template on to folded light blue fabric six times. This will give you twelve pieces. Sew six together for the front of the skirt and six together for the back, leaving an opening at one end on each for turning through. Set the back aside for now.

2 Tack (baste) the front skirt to the wadding (batting) to hold. Trim the wadding to match the front fabric. With the wadding in place a slightly quilted effect will be created when the appliqués are whipstitched in place.

3 Trace two of each snowflake and several dots on to the paper side of the freezer paper. Press the shiny side on to the wrong side of the white sparkle felt (see Tip below). Cut out on the lines. Peel the freezer paper off the felt and repeat. The freezer paper template will stick about six to eight times.

> ### >> TIP
> *When pressing freezer paper on to sparkle felt, press on to the wrong side of the felt. Some of the sparkle will pull off the felt if it is pressed on to the right side.*

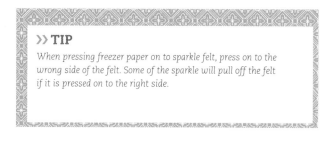

4 Glue or pin the snowflakes in place on the skirt
  front (the design is symmetrical). Dashed lines
indicate where pieces overlap. I started with one type of
snowflake, glueing them down and stitching them, and
then moved on to the next type of snowflake.

5 With one strand of blanc (white) stranded cotton,
  whipstitch the snowflakes in place. Use one strand
of white to sew the beads to the centres, points and
middle of dots on all appliquéd snowflakes.

6 To make the ruffle, cut the tulle or netting into 4in
  (10.2cm) strips. Fold in half along the length and
using one strip at a time, match the raw edges of the skirt
front and netting. Sew slowly with a tacking (basting)
stitch, pushing pleats or gathers into the stitch. It can be
difficult to keep all edges together so if the netting edges
go awry, just straighten them back. There is so no need
to sew the netting strips together, just pick up the next
strip and place it on top of the one finished. I used seven
strips. When you reach the opposite end, trim off excess.

7 For the skirt ties, pin a 12in (30.5cm) length of wired
  ribbon on to the open ends of the skirt front at the
points marked with X on the template. Let ribbon extend
1in (2.5cm) over at X and 11in (27.9cm) on the front – this
will leave a length for strength. Tack (baste) in place.

8 With right sides together, pin the front and the back along all edges. Use lots of pins and smooth out often, checking that raw edges and seams match on all curves at the top and bottom. Make sure the ribbon lengths will not get caught in the seam by pinning them together in the inside. Sew, starting on the open straight edge. Leave an opening between the middle and bottom ribbon along one straight edge for turning. Sew all other edges. Do not trim at the ribbons – leave extra length so that they do not pull out when tied. Trim all fabric and wadding and clip corners to remove excess bulk.

9 Reach inside and remove the pins at the ribbons. Now, pull the entire skirt right side out. Use a pencil end to push out the corners. Hand stitch the opening closed and press carefully using the sides and point of the iron. Do not press the netting as it may melt and avoid the beads. I also ironed from the back. Topstitch ¼in (6mm) from the edge all around to finish.

Seasonal Kitchen

The kitchen is a busy place in the winter season, filled with heady aromas and delicious delicacies. Handmade chocolates, cookies, cakes and preserves make welcome presents and whether you are baking to give as gifts or in preparation for a family Christmas feast, the projects in this chapter will add to your enjoyment.

Prepare for your culinary efforts and get into the festive spirit by donning a practical apron decorated with a sweet gingerbread house and gingerbread men. A collection of gorgeous gift baskets can be filled with delicious indulgences, while handmade tags will give gifts a personal touch.

The appliqué motifs in this chapter are in the form of gingerbread and candy canes, while colours are a mix of vibrant red, green and yellow, with warm ginger and snowy white for contrast. Hand embroidery adds charming finishing touches to all the designs.

Sweet Gift Tags

I've created four Christmas designs that can be used for gift tags – a gingerbread man, a gingerbread house, a candy cane and a heart. The motifs can be displayed on different coloured felts to create a useful range of tags. You could add paper to the inside for long notes or poems.

You will need...

For one tag

- Wool felt for outside in choice of colour (green, red, yellow or off-white) 4in x 8in (10.2cm x 20.3cm)

- Wool felt for rectangle front in choice of colour (green, red, yellow, white or off-white) 3in (7.6cm) square

- Wool felt for design 4in (10.2cm) square of each: ginger, white, pink and tan for the house; ginger for the man; white for the candy cane and red and pink for the heart

- Heavyweight craft paper

- Satin ribbon ⅛in (3mm) wide x 18in (45.7cm) long

- Freezer paper

- Craft glue

- Hole punch tool

- Large-eyed needle for ribbon

- DMC stranded cotton (floss): 470 green, 3777 red, 869 brown, 310 black, 223 pink and blanc (white), plus colours to match wool felts

Finished size (folded):
3in x 3½in (7.6cm x 8.8cm)

›› Directions

1 See the Template section for the relevant templates. Cut one scalloped outside from your choice of wool felt colour as follows. Trace the scallop shape on to the paper side of the freezer paper, press the shiny side of the paper on to wool felt and cut out on the line. Peel off the paper.

2 Cut out a rectangle for the front of the tag in your colour choice 2¼in x 2¾in (5.7cm x 7cm). Your appliqué shape will go on this piece.

3 Prepare your appliqué motif. Trace the design on to the paper side of the freezer paper. Press the shiny side down on to wool felt and cut out the shape on the design line. For the candy cane, cut one from white felt. For the heart, cut one scallop from pink felt and one heart from red felt. For the gingerbread

man, cut one from brown felt. For the house, cut one house from brown felt (note where the house goes under the icing on the design layout). Cut one icing roof from white felt, cut one scallop for a door from pink felt and cut one door from tan felt.

4 Use spots of glue to hold the appliqué shapes in place on your rectangle. Use one strand of matching embroidery thread to whipstitch down. Now work the embroidery as described in the panel.

5 Using spots of glue or pins attach the finished rectangle to the scallop outside. Using one strand of matching embroidery thread, whipstitch the rectangle in place. Press the scallop outside in half at the fold.

6 Cut a piece of heavyweight paper 2½in x 3in (6.3cm x 7.6cm) for inside the tag. Make a hole with a hole punch ¼in (6mm) down and in the middle of one short side. Fold the ribbon in half, matching the ends. Bring the loop through the hole in the paper, thread the ends of the ribbon through the loop and pull, creating a tassel. Thread one ribbon end into a large-eyed needle and pull the ribbon from the inside to the outside scallop at the fold marked X on the template. Do the same with the other ribbon end. Write a note or poem in your tag to finish.

›› Embroidery

- Candy cane: use three strands of red embroidery cotton (floss) to straight stitch the lines. (1)
- Heart: use three strands of pink for French knot dots on scallop. (2)
- Gingerbread man: use two strands of white for backstitch icing on arms and legs and French knot buttons. Use two strands of black for French knot eyes. (3)
- House: use three strands of brown for a French knot door knob. Use three strands of pink for French knot dots on the door scallop. (4)
- All designs: use three strands of red to work French knot holly berries on the rectangle. Use two strands of green to straight stitch pine needles at each berry. (5)

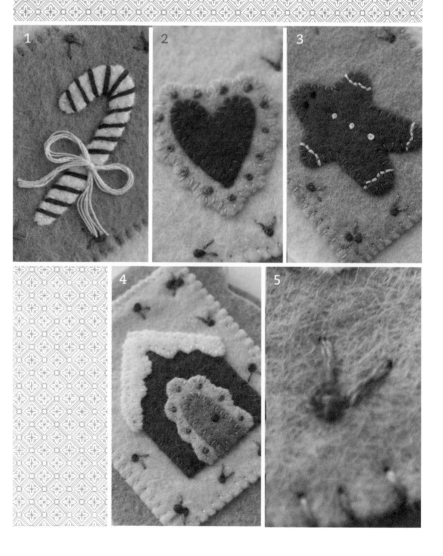

Sweet Treat Baskets

A charming basket makes a lovely gift all on its own or filled with homemade goodies. The instructions describe the larger gingerbread house basket, but also include measurements and details for medium and small baskets (see picture at the end of the chapter).

You will need...

For one basket

- Off-white or muslin fabric ¼yd (0.25m)

- Print fabric for basket outside and strap (red, yellow or green) ¼yd (0.25m)

- Lightweight quilt wadding (batting) 9in x 28in (23cm x 71cm)

- Craft-weight interfacing (fusible on one side preferable) 9in x 28in (23cm x 71cm)

- Medium-weight fusible interfacing (optional) ¼yd (0.25m)

- Freezer paper

- Craft glue

- Two buttons 1in (2.5cm) diameter and two ½in (1.3cm) diameter

- Ginger brown wool felt 9in (23cm) square

- White wool felt 6in (15.2cm) square

- Red wool felt 4in (10.2cm) square

- Wool felt for gingerbread house in pink, tan, yellow and green 4in (10.2cm) square of each

- DMC stranded cotton (floss): 470 green, 3777 red, 3830 light red, 869 brown, 310 black, 223 pink, 3821 yellow and blanc (white), plus colours to match wool felt colours

Finished sizes:

Large: 6½in x 6½in (16.5cm x 16.5cm)

Medium: 6½in x 4½in (16.5cm x 11.4cm)

Small: 6½in x 3½in (16.5cm x 8.9cm)

» Directions

1 See the Template section for the relevant templates. The baskets are all the same diameter but different heights. Cut one circle base for the basket outside from print fabric. Cut out on the solid line (the size given is the cutting line). Mark on four sides as shown on the template. Back with wadding (batting) cut the same size. Tack (baste) to the fabric to hold if desired (or use spray basting glue). Cut one base from craft-weight interfacing cut ½in (1.3cm) smaller and fuse to the wadding leaving ¼in (6mm) all around for a seam. Set this piece aside for now.

» TIP

If you do not have fusible craft-weight interfacing, make some by fusing some fusible web to one side of the interfacing.

2 For the large house basket, cut one outside from print fabric 7in x 20½in (17.8cm x 52cm). Back with a piece of wadding (batting) cut the same size. Centre on to the wrong side of the outside side piece.

For the medium size gingerbread man basket use a 5in x 20½in (12.7cm x 52cm) piece, backed with wadding.

For the smaller candy cane basket use a 4in x 20½in (10.2cm x 52cm) piece, backed with wadding.

3 Use the templates to cut out the appliqué pieces for the basket. There are three gingerbread houses for the large basket, five gingerbread men for the medium basket and ten candy canes for the small basket. Trace the appliqué pieces on to the paper side of the freezer paper. Trace one of each and reuse your freezer paper templates. Press the shiny side of the freezer paper on to the wool felt and cut out on the line. Pull the paper shape off and press again.

For the house on the large basket: use the templates to cut the wool felt pieces necessary for three houses. From ginger brown felt cut roof pieces and a house piece. From white felt cut the icing under the roof, the candy canes and the candies on the sides of the house. From pink felt cut the window scallop, door scallop and cupcake frosting. From tan felt cut the door, window and cupcake bottom. From red felt cut the heart, the cherry for the cupcake and two gumdrops. From green felt cut two gumdrops and from yellow felt cut three gumdrops. Lay the pieces on your prepared 7in x 20½in (17.8cm x 52cm) strip and use dots of glue to hold in place.

For the gingerbread men on the medium basket: use the templates to cut five gingerbread men from ginger brown felt. Cut five hearts from red felt. Lay on your prepared 5in x 20½in (12.7cm x 52cm) strip and use dots of glue to hold in place.

For the candy canes on the small basket: use the templates to cut ten candy canes from white felt. Cross two

canes, using a dot of glue. Make five sets of two candy canes. Lay on your prepared 4in x 20½in (10.2cm x 52cm) strip and use dots of glue to hold in place.

4 Using one strand of embroidery cotton matching the felt colours, whipstitch the appliqués in place. Now work the embroidery as described in the panel.

5 Back the appliquéd piece with craft-weight interfacing cut 6½in x 20in (16.5cm x 50.8cm) for the house basket. Fuse to the wrong side leaving ¼in (6mm) all around.

For the gingerbread man basket cut a piece of interfacing 4½in x 20in (11.4cm x 50.8cm) and fuse.

For the candy canes basket cut a piece of interfacing 3½in x 20in (8.9cm x 50.8cm) and fuse.

TIP

To cut out candies and cherries for the gingerbread house, use a ¼in (6mm) diameter hole punch tool. Punch the wool felt and use the dot for the candy or cherry.

›› Embroidery

- Houses: with three strands of red embroidery cotton, straight stitch the candy cane stripes and the cherry stem. Work French knot dots around the heart and dots on the red gumdrops. With one strand of red, work stripes on the candies. With three strands of pink, work French knot dots on the cupcake icing, dots on the door scallop and window scallop. With three strands of brown, backstitch the window panes and the cupcake base and a French knot door knob. (1)
- Gingerbread men: use three strands of black for French knot eyes. Use two strands of white for backstitch icing on arms and legs. Use three strands of white for French knot buttons. (2)
- Candy canes: use three strands of red for straight stitch stripes. For the bow use four strands of green, bringing your threaded needle down on one side of the candy canes and up on the other where they meet at the criss-cross. Leave tails of thread 5in (12.7cm) long on each side and tie into a bow. Use tiny spots of glue to hold the bow at the knot. Once dry, cut the tails to 1in (2.5cm) long. (3)

6 Begin to assemble the basket as follows. Make a mark along the bottom of the strip with a wash-away marker or pencil, marking the middle at 10¼in (26cm) and at 5in (12.7cm) on each side of this mark. The seam will be the fourth mark to match the circle base. With right sides together, sew the appliqué piece into a circle along the 7in (17.8cm) side. Press the seam open.

For the gingerbread man basket sew along the 5in (12.7cm) side.

For the candy cane basket sew along the 4in (10.2cm) side.

7 With right sides together, pin the base to the side strip, matching the marks on the circle to the marks on the strip. Make sure you are pinning the bottom edge to the circle base. Sew ¼in (6mm) all around. Turn right side out.

along the scallop (the solid line on the template). Trim, clip into the point of the scallop, turn through and press the scallops well.

11 With right sides together, pin the muslin circle base to this scalloped muslin piece along the bottom straight edge. Sew, catching all fabric edges in the seam. Press but do not turn right side out. Put the muslin piece into the appliquéd piece, wrong sides together. Make sure the seams match and that the bottom muslin base is all the way inside, against the outside base. Turn the scallop down to the outside. Check under the fold to make sure the outside edge is up against the fold to catch in the topstitching. When you are sure everything is all lined up, sew ¼ in (6mm) from the top through all layers.

8 From muslin cut one circle base for inside the basket and mark as shown at the four points. Set aside for now. For the house basket cut two pieces from muslin 8¼ in x 20½ in (21cm x 52cm).
For the gingerbread man basket cut two pieces 6¼ in x 20½ in (15.9cm x 52cm).
For the candy cane basket cut two pieces 5¼ in x 20½ in (13.3cm x 52cm).
Back one of these pieces with interfacing cut 8in x 20in (20.3cm x 50.8cm) (or 6in/15.2cm or 5in/12.7cm), leaving ¼ in (6mm) all around. Trace the scallop on the piece with the interfacing ¼ in (6mm) from the top edge.

9 Trace the stitching lines for the pine needle vine and work the embroidery. With two strands of green embroidery cotton, backstitch the vine and pine needles. With three strands of light red, work French knot berries.

10 Mark this embroidered muslin piece at the middle and at 5in (12.7cm) on each side of middle along the bottom (the opposite side of the embroidered vine). The seam will be the fourth mark. Cut the scallop along the cutting line. Sew into a circle along the 8¼ in (21cm) length (or the 6¼ in/15.9cm length or the 5¼ in/13.3cm length). Press the seam open. Do not turn right side out. Sew the remaining muslin strip into a circle and press the seam open. Turn right side out. Place the muslin pieces right sides together and sew along the top

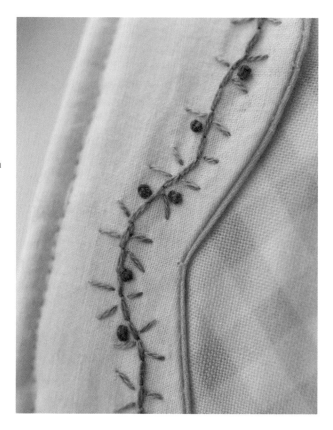

12 To make the handle, cut a strip from print fabric 2¾in x 16in (7cm x 40.6cm). With right sides together sew along the 16in (40.6cm) length and then turn right side out. Cut a strip 1in x 15½in (2.5cm x 39.4cm) from craft-weight interfacing. Work the interfacing into the strap leaving ¼in (6mm) on each end free. Turn in the ends ¼in (6mm) neatly on each side and press well. Topstitch ⅛in (3mm) all around.

13 Make a button stack with a 1in (2.5cm) button and ½in (1.3cm) button. Sew the button stack through all layers on the outside of the basket at the seam and another stack on the opposite side to hold the strap in place. Fill with cookies to finish.

The gift basket can be made in different sizes and two different versions are shown here. They are made in the same way as the house basket. One is decorated with gingerbread men appliqués on a yellow print fabric and the other has candy canes on a pale green print.

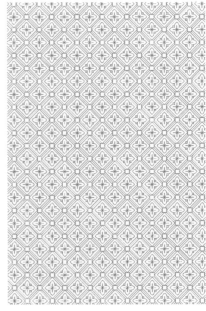

Gingerbread Apron

This useful apron has a lovely retro feel and is very straightforward to make. It is decorated with two appliqué designs, a gingerbread house and gingerbread man, but you could use other Christmas motifs from the book.

You will need...

- Red plaid (check) fabric for apron front ¾yd (0.75m)
- Green print fabric for apron bottom flounce 1yd (1m)
- Red print for 'house' pocket ¼yd (0.25m)
- Yellow plaid (check) fabric for two 'gingerbread man' pockets and the ties ½yd (0.5m)
- Medium-weight interfacing ¼yd (0.25m)
- Freezer paper
- Craft glue
- White ric-rac braid ⅝in (1.6cm) wide x 7yd (6½m)
- Ginger brown wool felt 10in (25.4cm) square
- White wool felt 6in (15.2cm) square
- Red wool felt 4in (10.2cm) square
- Wool felt for gingerbread house 4in (10.2cm) square each of pink, tan, yellow and green
- DMC stranded cotton (floss): 470 green, 3777 red, 3830 light red, 869 brown, 310 black, 223 pink, 3821 yellow and blanc (white), plus colours to match wool felt colours
- Spray starch for pressing

Finished size:

30½in (80cm) long x 27in (68.6cm) at waistband, excluding ties

›› Directions

1   See the Template section for the relevant templates. Cut the front for the apron on the solid line from red plaid fabric on the fold. Seam allowances and hems are included on the pattern. Cut one bottom piece on the solid line from green print fabric on the fold. See Fig 1 for the apron layout.

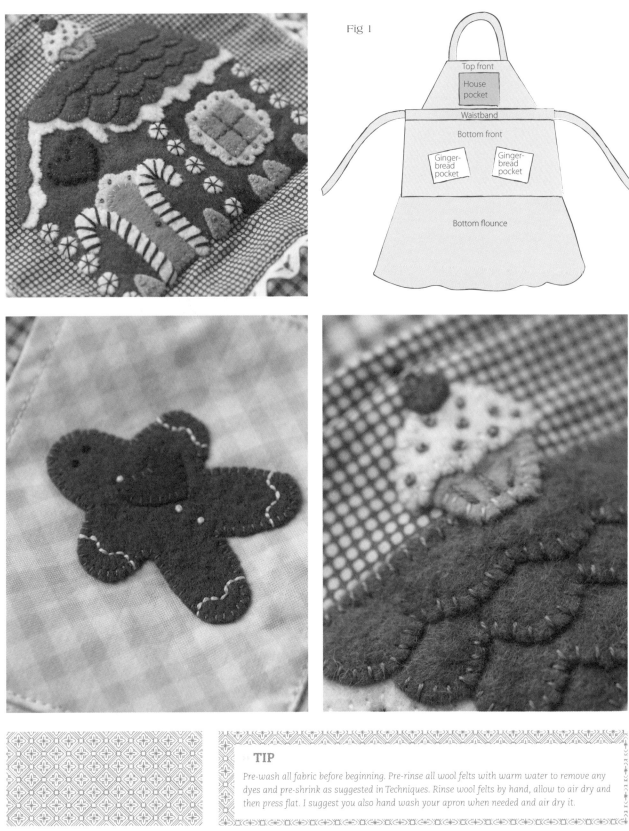

Fig 1

Top front

House pocket

Waistband

Bottom front

Gingerbread pocket

Gingerbread pocket

Bottom flounce

TIP

Pre-wash all fabric before beginning. Pre-rinse all wool felts with warm water to remove any dyes and pre-shrink as suggested in Techniques. Rinse wool felts by hand, allow to air dry and then press flat. I suggest you also hand wash your apron when needed and air dry it.

2 Sew the pieces together with French seams as follows. With wrong sides together, pin the bottom flounce to the front along the bottom of the front and short curve on the flounce. Sew a ¼ in (6mm) seam. Press to one side and trim to ⅛in (3mm). Turn to right sides together and sew ¼ in (6mm) seam. Press towards the flounce.

3 Cut ric-rac braid to fit across this seam, plus ½ in (1.3cm) extending on each side. Tack (baste) the ric-rac in place to hold temporarily. This will be embroidered later.

4 Turn down the edges. Press ¼ in (6mm) on all selvedge edges to the wrong side. Press the arm edges, top, sides and along the bottom, turning the ric-rac at the flounce into this hem. Turn down again along the top only ½ in (1.3cm) to the wrong side. Turn down again along the arms, sides and bottom ¼ in (6mm) to the wrong side. Spray starch these hems to hold them well.

5 To make the strap for the head, cut a strip from green print 2¾ in x 23in (7cm x 58.4cm). Fold in half along the length, right sides together, and sew a ¼ in (6mm) seam. Turn right side out and press. Turn under the ends by ¼ in (6mm) to the inside strap to finish. Spray starch to hold crisply. Topstitch along the length on both sides.

6 Pin the strap in place along the top to hold temporarily. Cut one ric-rac strip the length of the top edge plus 1in (2.5cm) on each side. Place along the top, allowing half of the ric-rac to show from the front and tack (baste) in place to hold. Turn ½ in (1.3cm) extending on each side into the hem edges on the arms. Now cut one ric-rac strip the length of the bottom edge plus 1in (2.5cm). Pin in place along the front, allowing half of the ric-rac to show and letting ½ in (1.3cm) extend from each edge. Tack into place. Turn the excess ½ in (1.3cm) of ric-rac into the hem on the sides.

7 Topstitch the apron on all edges. Start with the top, topstitching ⅜ in (1cm) from the top. Topstitch the arms, sides and bottom just under ¼ in (6mm) to catch all hems and the ric-rac.

8 To make the waistband casing, cut one strip from green print 3½ in x 27½ in (8.9cm x 69.8cm). Turn ¼ in (6mm) along the length on both sides to the wrong side, and repeat. Turn ¼ in (6mm) at the short ends to the wrong side, press, and repeat. Check the fit. This should match the sides when lying across the front, where shown. There is extra length given to work with on the waistband, so turn the ends out or in if necessary to fit. Spray starch to hold the hems crisply. Topstitch along the short ends.

9 Pin the waistband casing to the apron front. Cut two ric-rac strips plus ½in (1.3cm) and pin in place allowing half of the ric-rac to show on the front to hold along the length of the casing on both edges. Tack in place. Turn ¼in (6mm), extending from the edges under itself. Topstitch the casing ⅛in (3mm) along the length, catching the casing and the ric-rac to hold. Repeat on the other side.

10 To make the pockets, use the templates and cut four pockets on the dashed line (the solid line is the sewing line) from yellow print and two from interfacing for the pockets on the hips. Cut two pockets on the dashed line (the solid line is sewing line) from red print and one from interfacing for the pocket on the top front. Cut out on the dashed line. Back two yellow pockets with interfacing cut to match. Back one red pocket with interfacing. Set the remaining fabric pockets aside for now.

11 Cut the appliqué pieces for the pockets and the flounce as follows. There are fourteen candy canes, two gingerbread men and one gingerbread house. For the candy canes on the flounce cut fourteen canes from white wool felt. Use the template as a guide and a dot of glue and criss-cross two to make seven sets of two canes. Position on your flounce, using dots of glue to hold.

For the gingerbread men on the yellow pockets, cut two men from ginger brown wool felt. Cut two hearts from red wool felt. Use the template as a guide and position these on your interfaced pocket fronts. Use dots of glue to hold in place.

For the gingerbread house, cut the pieces necessary. Cut roof pieces and a house piece from ginger brown wool felt. Cut icing under the roof, candy canes and candies on the sides of the house from white felt. Cut the window scallop, door scallop and cupcake frosting from pink felt. Cut the door, window and cupcake bottom from tan felt. Cut the heart, cherry for the cupcake and two gumdrops from red felt. Cut two gumdrops from green felt and three gumdrops from yellow felt. Use dots of glue to hold the pieces in place and then dots of glue to hold the complete house on your interfaced red pocket.

12 Using one strand of embroidery cotton (floss) that matches wool felt colours, whipstitch all the appliqués in place. Now work the embroidery on the apron appliqués as described in the panel.

13 With right sides together, sew the pockets to their matching pieces set aside earlier. Sew ¼in (6mm) all around, leaving an opening for turning 2in (5cm) wide along the straight edge bottom. Clip corners, turn through and press. Slipstitch the opening closed.

14 Pin the pockets to the apron where shown on the pattern. Cut ric-rac to go around each

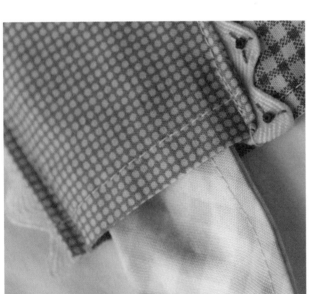

TIP

To cut out candies and cherry for cupcake on the house, use a ¼in (6mm) hole punch tool. Punch the wool felt and use the dot for the candy or cherry.

pocket plus ¼ in (6mm) extending along the top. Turn the ric-rac at the top under and tack in place under the pockets, allowing half of the ric-rac to show on the front. Topstitch the pockets in place with ⅛ in (3mm) stitch, catching the pockets and ric-rac from the top corner to the opposite top corner, leaving the top free.

15 Embroider the ric-rac using three strands of light red embroidery cotton for French knot berries on the ric-rac edges exposed on pockets, casing and flounce. Use two strands of green to backstitch the vine and straight stitch pine needles.

16 To make the apron ties, cut two strips of yellow print 4in (10.2cm) x the width of the fabric (44in/112cm). Sew along the 4in (10.2cm) side, right sides together, to create a strip about 87in (220cm) long. Fold in half right sides together along the length. Sew ¼ in (6mm) across the end, pivot and sew along the length to about the middle seam. Leave 4in (10.2cm) open and continue sewing along the length to the opposite end, pivot and sew the opposite end closed. Using a safety pin or bodkin, turn the strip right side out, pulling each end through the hole left in the middle. Clip the corners, press flat and slipstitch the opening closed. Topstitch ¼ in (6mm) along all edges. Work the tie through the waistband casing to finish your apron.

›› Embroidery

- Candy canes: use three strands of red embroidery cotton to straight stitch stripes. Using four strands of green thread, bring your threaded needle down on one side of the candy canes and up on the other where they meet at the criss-cross. Leave thread tails 5in (12.7cm) long on each side and tie into a bow. Use tiny spots of glue to hold the bow at the knot. Allow to dry and cut the tails to 1in (2.5cm) long. (1)
- Gingerbread men: use three strands of black for French knot eyes. Use two strands of white for backstitch icing on arms and legs. Use three strands of white for French knot buttons. (2)
- Gingerbread house: use three strands of red for straight stitch candy cane stripes and cherry stem. Work French knot dots around the heart and on the red gumdrops. Use one strand of red for stripes on the candies. Use three strands of pink for French knot dots on the cupcake icing, dots on the door scallop and window scallop. Use three strands of brown and backstitch for windowpanes and cupcake base and a French knot for the door knob. Use three strands of green for French knot dots on the green gumdrops and three strands of yellow for the French knots on the yellow gumdrops. (3)

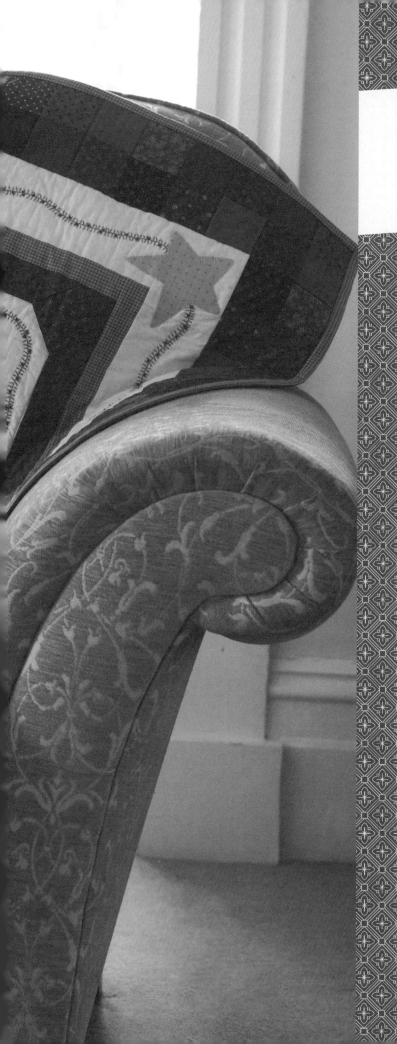

Christmas Night

The night before Christmas is a magical time, especially for children excitedly trying to sleep while secretly listening for Santa to arrive. For us grown-ups it's more of a hectic dash to finish all the gift wrapping and house decorating.

Make Christmas night extra special with a festive pillowcase with a star appliqué – perfect for Christmas night dreaming. Hanging up the Christmas stocking is a tradition for most of us on Christmas night and the stocking in this chapter has Santa making his way through the night sky. On the most exciting night of the year, a cosy quilt will warm your lap when all is calm. Fun designs conjure the spirit of the season.

Lots of festive reds, greens and yellows were used for the projects, with polka dot fabrics giving the appearance of snow. Prints with small motifs allow the appliqué and embroidery to shine.

3 hour project

Star Pillowcase

Christmas night will be made extra special with this pillowcase to sleep on or put extra presents in! The yellow stars contrast well with the Christmas red fabric used.

You will need...

- Red fabric for stocking ¾yd (0.75m)
- Off-white fabric for cuff ¼yd (0.25m)
- Green fabric for accent trim 2in x 44in (5cm x 111.8cm)
- Yellow fabric for stars ⅛yd (12cm)
- Fusible web
- Embroidery cotton (floss) in yellow to match star fabric

Finished size:
30in x 20in
(76.2cm x 50.8cm)

>> **Directions**

1 Cut the selvedges from the green, off-white and red pillowcase fabrics. Lay the off-white fabric out to length (44in/111.8cm). With a wash-away fabric marker, mark the centre length at 22in (55.9cm). Mark the centre width at 4½in (11.4cm). Make a line to mark the centre width from the left edge to the middle length (see Fig 1).

Fig 1

Mark centre of
width and length

2 See the Template section for the relevant templates. Trace three stars on to the paper side of the fusible web. Press the stars on to the wrong side of the yellow fabric and cut them out. Press the stars on to the off-white cuff piece, on the left side at the top as in Fig 2. Avoid the seam by placing them ½in (1.3cm) from raw edge or over the drawn middle lines. Whipstitch in place using one strand of yellow embroidery cotton.

Fig 2

3 Fold the green accent fabric piece wrong sides together in half along the length and press. Lay out the off-white piece with stars. Lay the green accent piece on top of the off-white piece along the top edge (star side) and match raw edges. Open out the main red fabric and lay it on top of the cuff and accent fabric. All the long lengths should match. If they do not, trim so they are even. Pin along the edge to keep all edges together.

Fig 3

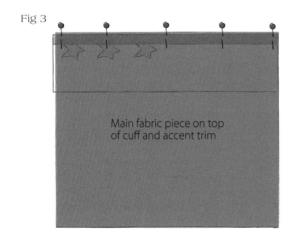

Main fabric piece on top
of cuff and accent trim

4 Starting at the opposite side of the pinned edge, roll the red fabric up into a tube up to the cuff, stopping the roll 2in (5cm) from the pinned edge (Fig 4). Now pick up the cuff and fold it over the roll, removing the pins one at a time. Re-pin, including the cuff edge just folded (there will be five layers of fabric now – cuff, two folded layers of trim, main fabric and cuff. Sew along the length through all layers. Reach into the tube at one end and pull out the main fabric. Press the cuff and accent fabric. Make sure the accent fabric is pressed towards the main fabric, so it will not go into your stars during the next step.

Fig 4

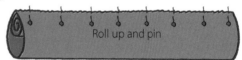

Roll up and pin

5 Fold in half with wrong sides together, matching cuff, accent and main fabric seams. Your piece is now approximately 22in x 30in (55.9cm x 76.2cm). Pin the raw edges and then sew along this L shape of raw edges. Trim the seam to a scant ⅛in (3mm). Turn inside out, so right sides are together and sew along the L shape again, creating finished French seams. Turn right side out and press to finish.

Sleigh Ride Stocking

What Christmas night is complete without that final hanging up of the stocking, filled with little goodies to be opened on Christmas morning? Try other motifs from the book to decorate stockings for the whole family.

You will need...

- Tan fabric for stocking front and back ½yd (0.5m)
- Three red and three green fabrics for toe and heel, each 3in x 6in (7.6cm x 15.2cm)
- Off-white flannel for cuff and lining ½yd (0.5m)
- Two yellow fabrics and one brown fabric for appliqué, each 8in (20.3cm) square
- Brown, black, red, white and muslin fabric for appliqué, each 4in (10.2cm) square
- Fusible web and medium-weight fusible interfacing
- Freezer paper
- Quilt wadding (batting) 18in (45.7cm) square
- DMC stranded embroidery cotton (floss): 310 black, 355 red, 433 brown, 469 green, 3821 yellow and blanc (white), plus colours to match appliqué fabrics

Finished size:
16in (40.6cm) tall x 12in (30.5cm) wide

» Directions

1 See the Template section for the relevant templates. Trace the stocking shape on the dashed line on to the paper side of the freezer paper. This is the cutting line. With the tan fabric folded wrong sides together, press the shiny side of the freezer paper on to the fabric. Cut out on the dashed line – because the fabric is folded this will create two shapes. (The solid line is the sewing line.) Peel the freezer paper off and keep it to use again.

2 Trace the embroidery and appliqué lines on to the front side of the stocking (the one with the toe pointed to the left). Tack (baste) the wadding (batting) to this stocking piece (or use a spray glue).

3 Cut fourteen 2½in (6.3cm) squares from the red and green fabrics chosen for the toe and heel. For the heel, sew eight together in alternating colours, two across and four down. For the toe, sew six together in alternating colours, two across and three down.

4 Using the templates and following the dashed line, trace the heel and toe piece on to the paper side of some freezer paper. Press the shiny side of the freezer paper on to the corresponding red/green patches. Cut out the shapes.

5 Turn under ¼in (6mm) on the curved side of the heel and toe where they are on the stocking

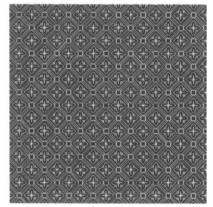

inside (not on the selvedge). Press this ¼in (6mm) well and pin in place. Using sewing thread, whipstitch a tiny seam to hold them in place along the turned-under edge.

6 Trace the appliqué pieces on to the paper side of the fusible web. The thick lines are appliqué and the thin lines are embroidery. A dashed line indicates where appliqué pieces overlap. Remember to reverse the tracing for designs that require a direction, such as the reindeer. After tracing each appliqué,

press on to the wrong side of the corresponding colours of fabrics.

7 Cut out the pieces and place where needed on the stocking. Trace any embroidery lines if required on to your appliqué pieces before pressing. Press to fuse with your iron. With a single strand of matching embroidery cotton, whipstitch the appliqués in place.

8 Using your freezer paper stocking shape, cut out two stockings from flannel, folding the flannel in half with wrong sides together. Set aside for now.

9 Trace the cuff on to the paper side of the freezer paper on the dashed line. Cut four cuffs from flannel folded wrong side together. Back one of these pieces with fusible interfacing cut ¼ in (6mm) smaller all around than the cuff.

10 On the piece of cuff backed with interfacing, trace the embroidery lines of the holly swag and the star placement. Trace three stars on to the paper side of the fusible web. Press the stars on to the wrong side of the yellow fabrics and cut out. Whipstitch the stars in place on the cuff with one strand of matching embroidery cotton. Now work the embroidery on the cuff and stocking as described in the panel.

›› Embroidery

- All embroidery is worked with two strands of embroidery cotton unless noted otherwise.
- Backstitch the holly scallops in green. Work the holly needles in green straight stitches. Work the berries in red French knots. (1)
- Work the reindeer eyes in black French knots, backstitch the sleigh rails and reins in black and the reindeer antlers and legs in brown. Lazy daisy stitch the reindeer ears and tails in brown and work a French knot for their noses. Backstitch the collars in red. Work French knot bells on the collars in yellow. (2)
- Lazy daisy stitch Santa's moustache with three strands of blanc (white). Work his eyes in black French knots. (3)

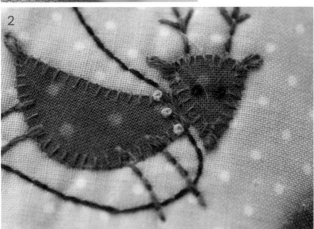

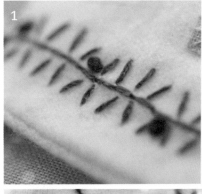

11 To make up the cuff, take the two cuff pieces and with right sides together, sew them together at the sides. Repeat for the other two. Press seams open. Place one cuff into the other cuff right sides together, matching scallops and seams. Sew along the scallop. Clip at the inside points of the curves, turn right side out and press well.

12 With right sides together, sew a tan stocking front to a matching stocking back all around, leaving the top open. Turn right side out and press.

13 With right sides together, sew two flannel stockings with a slightly larger seam than the tan stockings (⅜in/1cm). Leave a 5in (12.7cm) opening in the stocking. Start 1in (2.5cm) above the heel, leave open 5in (12.7cm) and continue sewing to the top of the stocking. Do not turn right side out.

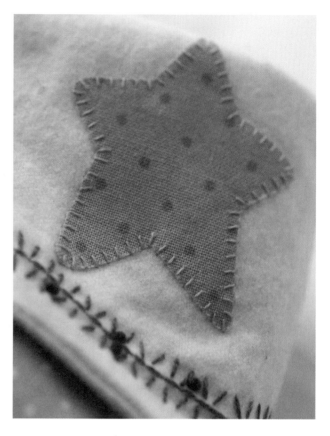

14 To make the tab hanger, cut a piece of flannel 1¾in x 6½in (4.4cm x 16.5cm). Turn under ¼in (6mm) to the wrong side on both long edges and press. Fold in half, wrong sides together, and topstitch along both long edges. Leave the ends undone.

15 Pin the cuff to the top of the stocking front with the star side matching the stocking front and matching seams. Fold the hanger in half and pin at the right-hand seam (the heel side). Tack (baste) through all layers all around the top. Put the outside stocking inside the flannel stocking (right sides together), matching seams. Pin around the top and sew all around twice. Reach into the opening in the flannel stocking and pull everything right side out. Push the flannel stocking to the inside of the front stocking and press along the top to finish.

Christmas Night Quilt

With all its festive reds, greens and golds, this quilt is perfect to celebrate Christmas.
Hang it on the wall as a decoration or use it as a cozy lap quilt.

You will need...

- Main red fabric ⅝yd (0.6m)
- Main green fabric ½yd (0.5m)
- Muslin for borders ½yd (0.5m)
- Tan fabric for centre blocks ⅓yd (0.3m)
- Four red fabrics for outer border ¼yd (0.25m) each
- Four green fabrics for outer border ¼yd (0.25m) each
- Brown fabric for inside border ¼yd (0.25m)
- Two yellow fabrics for appliqué, 12in (30.5cm) square each
- Appliqué fabrics: six green, three brown, two blue, one white, orange, grey, black, muslin and off-white flannel, each 10in (25.4cm) square
- Fusible web 2yd (2m)
- Backing fabric 2¼yd (2.25m)
- Quilt wadding (batting) 54in (137cm) square
- Binding fabric ½yd (0.5m)
- DMC stranded embroidery cotton (floss): 310 black, 355 red, 433 brown, 469 green, 580 light green, 646 grey, 926 blue, 976 orange, 3821 yellow and blanc (white), plus colours to match appliqué fabrics

Finished size:
47in x 47in (119.4cm x 119.4cm)

›› Directions

1 Cut one strip of tan fabric for the centre blocks 10½in (26.7cm) x width of fabric. Subcut these strips into four 10½in (26.7cm) squares.
Cut two muslin strips 2in (5cm) x width of fabric and subcut these into thirty-two 2in (5cm) squares.
Cut four muslin strips 2in (5cm) x width of fabric and subcut these into sixteen 10½in (26.7cm) strips.

Cut four red strips 2in (5cm) x width of fabric and subcut these into sixteen 10½in (26.7cm) strips.

Cut two green strips 3½in (8.9cm) x width of fabric and subcut these into sixteen 3½in (8.9cm) squares.

Cut three red strips 2in (5cm) x width of fabric and subcut these into forty-eight 2in (5cm) squares.

For borders cut four brown strips 1½in (3.8cm) x width of fabric. Cut four muslin strips 3½in (8.9cm) x width of fabric. For the four-patch outer border cut ten strips of red and green fabrics, each 2½in (6.3cm) x width of fabric.

2 Start by making the centre blocks. Create the corner triangles by sewing a 2in (5cm) muslin square to each tan 10½in (26.7cm) square as shown in Fig 1A–D. Place the tan square right side up and the muslin square right side down, aligning corners. Sew across the muslin square on the diagonal. Trim the seam to ¼in (6mm) and then press the corner open. Repeat on the other three corners to finish with a block as shown in Fig 1E. Make four blocks like this.

3 Prepare the borders for each centre block using the same technique described in step 2. Sew three red 2in (5cm) squares on the diagonal to green 3½in (8.9cm) squares. Sew one muslin 2in (5cm) square on the diagonal to the remaining corner (Fig 2). Trim seams to ¼in (6mm) and press the seam open. Make sixteen units like this.

Fig 1 Creating triangle corners on the centre blocks

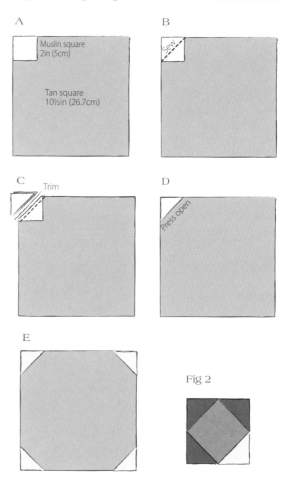

Fig 2

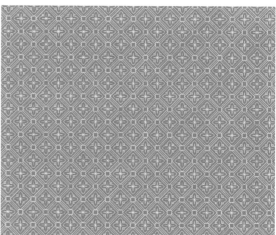

4 Now sew a muslin 2in x 10½in (5cm x 26.7cm) strip to a red 2in x 10½in (5cm x 26.7cm) strip along the 10½in (26.7cm) length. Press open. Make sixteen 3½in x 10½in (8.9cm x 26.7cm) units in this way.

5 Sew a muslin/red strip to the sides of each 10½in (26.7cm) centre block (see Fig 3). Sew the muslin side to the centre block, right sides together and press open. You will use eight of the muslin/red strips.

6 Sew a corner square to the remaining muslin/red strips. With right sides together, match the muslin corner of a square to the muslin side of the strip on both sides. Press open.

7 Sew these strips with corners on to the top and bottom of the centre blocks, right sides together and press open (Fig 3). Each centre block should be 16½in (42cm) square. Now sew the four centre blocks together in a four-patch arrangement.

8 The inner border can now be added to the quilt top. Sew brown strips 1½in x 32½in (3.8cm x 82.5cm) to the sides and press open. Sew brown strips 1½in x 34½in (3.8cm x 87.6cm) to the top and bottom and press open.

9 Now add the middle border. Sew 3½in x 34½in (8.9cm x 87.6cm) muslin strips to the sides and press open. Sew 3½in x 40½in (8.9cm x 103cm) muslin strips to the top and bottom and press open.

10 Add the outer four-patch border as follows. Place a 2½in (6.3cm) wide x width of fabric red strip right sides together with a green strip the same size, and sew together along the length (Fig 4A). Press the seam to the green side on the wrong side as you press open. Sew ten sets of the two colours. Lay the combination strip horizontally on your cutting mat and subcut these strips into 2½in (6.3cm) widths. Sew two together to create a 4½in (11.4cm) four-patch square, with alternating red and green (Fig 4B). You will need twenty-four of these units.

Fig 3 Bordering the centre blocks

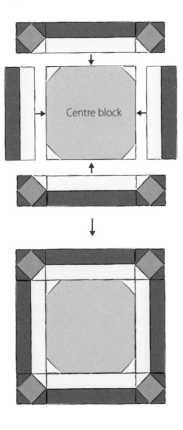

Centre block

Fig 4 Making four-patch units

A

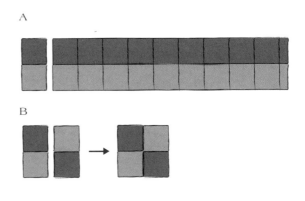

B

11 Sew ten four-patch blocks together to fit the side of the quilt top (make two). Sew these right sides together on each side and press open (see Fig 5A).

12 Sew twelve four-patch blocks together for the top and bottom of the quilt (make two). Sew these right sides together on the top and bottom and press open. Fig 5B shows the layout of the finished quilt top.

Fig 5

A

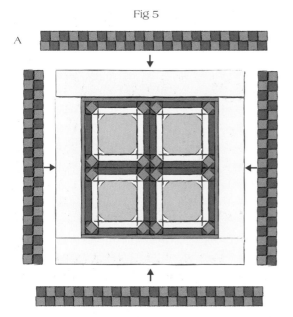

B

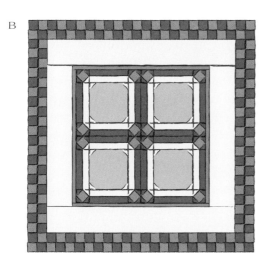

13 Your quilt is now ready to be embellished. See the Template section for the relevant templates. Trace the design of each block and border on to the quilt top with a wash-away pen or pencil. Trace the appliqué pieces on to the paper side of the fusible web. Thick lines on the templates indicate appliqué and thin lines show embroidery. A dashed line indicates where appliqué pieces overlap. Remember to reverse the tracing for designs that require a direction, such as the reindeer.

14 After tracing each individual appliqué, press on to the wrong side of the corresponding colours of fabrics. Cut out the pieces and place where needed on the central blocks (see photos). Trace embroidery lines on to your appliqué pieces before pressing. Press to hold with your iron. With one strand of matching embroidery cotton, whipstitch the appliqués in place.

15 Back the quilt with wadding (batting) at this point to create a quilted effect while stitching. Tack (baste) the quilt to the wadding or use safety pins or spray glue. Work the embroidery on the quilt as described in the panel.

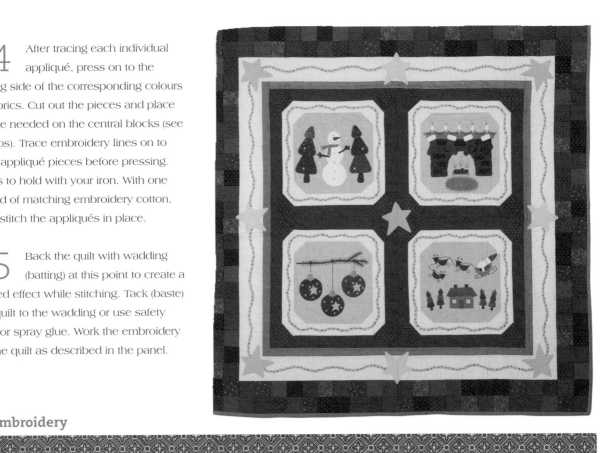

›› Embroidery

- All embroidery is worked with two strands of embroidery cotton unless noted otherwise.
- Backstitch all vines in green. Straight stitch needles in green. Work berries in red French knots. (1)
- Snowman block: use three strands for the white embroidery. Backstitch the snow along the bottom in white. Straight stitch the snowflakes in white. Use black French knots for the eyes, mouth and buttons. Work blue French knots on the ends of the scarf with the fringe straight stitched in blue. (2)
- Fireplace block: straight stitch the V on the candle flames in orange. Backstitch the lines on the fireplace flames in orange. Backstitch the log stand in black. Straight stitch the candlewicks with one strand of black. Work French knot dots on the rug and straight stitch the fringe in blue. (3)
- Ornament block: work pine needles in straight stitches with three strands of light green. Work snowflakes on ornaments in straight stitches with three strands of white. Backstitch the ornament loops in grey. Use black to backstitch the ornament strings, to lazy daisy stitch bows at the top and straight stitch the bow ends. Add French knot dots at star points in yellow. (4)
- Santa and reindeer block: use black to work French knots for all eyes and backstitch sleigh rails and reindeer reins. Backstitch the reindeer collars in red. Work French knot bells on the collars in yellow. Use brown to backstitch the reindeer antlers and legs and the windowpanes. Use brown to work lazy daisy stitches for the ears and tails. Work French knots noses in brown. Lazy daisy stitch Santa's moustache with three strands of white. Work French knot lights on the house in alternating red, green, and yellow. (5)

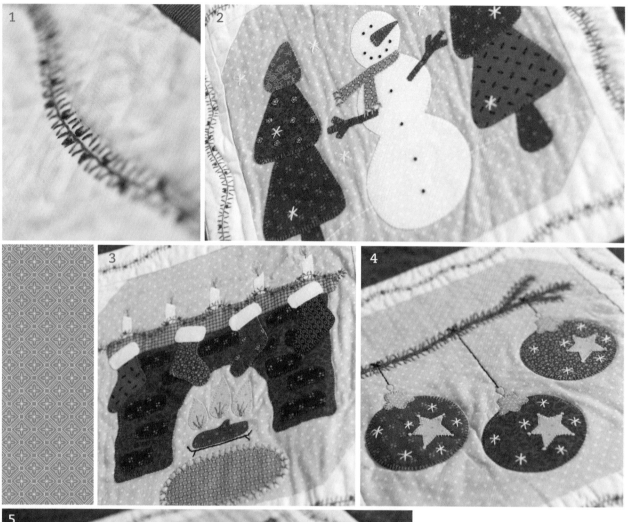

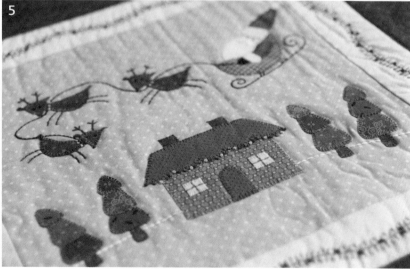

16 Use your backing fabric to back the quilt. You could quilt further at this stage if desired, for example, machine quilting in the seam ditches and in the outer border and echo quilting around the appliqué motifs. Bind the quilt to finish – see Binding in Basic Techniques.

Holiday Party

please join us for a holiday party
hosted by

THE ANDERSON FAMILY
december 18th at 7:00pm
at our home

rsvp to mary by december the 1st

festive attire and hearty appetites
greatly encouraged

Holiday Party

please join us for a holiday party hosted by

THE ANDERSON FAMILY
december 18th at 7:00pm
at our home

rsvp to mary by december the 1st

festive attire and hearty appetites greatly encouraged

Holiday Party

join us for a holiday party
hosted by

E ANDERSON FAMILY
cember 18th at 7:00pm
at our home

mary by december the 1st

attire and hearty appetites
greatly encouraged

Christmas Party

For many people Christmas time is one
long party season – sometimes starting
before Christmas Eve and continuing
into New Year! This chapter gives ideas
on making your party go with a swing.

The projects begin with customized party
invitations, and whether you hand write
the invitations or type them in a special-
occasion font they will make your guests
feel special. A range of decorations
complete with stars and ribbons could
be used on the Christmas tree or be tied
around napkins on a party table. A lush
garland brings back childhood memories
of paper chains and would look gorgeous
hanging in swags from a buffet table.

I have used mostly white, silver and gold
to make this range of elegant projects.
Iridescent fabrics and sparkly netting
create a party atmosphere and the
stars are both festive and celebratory.

 3 hour project

Party Invitations

Start a Christmas party in style with these lovely invitations, which can be typed or hand written. I have created four different invitations to show how you can vary the design.

You will need...

For four invitations

- White or antique white wool felt 10in x 26in (25.4cm x 66cm)
- Wool felt in white, off-white, gold and grey (silver) 4in (10.2cm) square each
- Four sheets of card stock paper (80lb/216gsm) in white or antique white
- Freezer paper
- Glue stick
- Tulle or bridal netting in gold and silver ½yd (0.5m) of 54in (137cm) wide each
- Ribbon in gold and silver ⅛in (3mm) wide x 1yd (1m) of each
- Four off-white buttons ⅜in (1cm) diameter
- DMC stranded cotton (floss): 646 grey and 832 gold

Finished size:
7¼in x 5¾in (18.4cm x 14.6cm) excluding netting

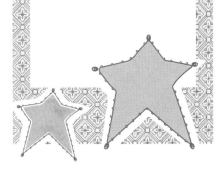

›› Directions

1 Cut the card stock paper sheets into 7in x 5½in (17.8cm x 14cm) and set aside for now. Cut the white or antique white wool felt 7¼in x 5¾in (18.4cm x 14.6cm). This will allow a ⅛in (3mm) overhang on every side of your sheet of card stock paper.

2 See the Template section for the relevant templates. Trace or transfer the designs on to wool felt and work the embroidery as described in the panel.

›› Embroidery

- All French knots are worked with three strands of stranded cotton.
- All lazy daisy stitches, all little stars and all running stitches are worked with two strands.
- See the photographs for the alternate designs and colours. For example, dots in gold have lazy daisy stitches in grey and running stitches in gold. Little stars in grey have running stitches in gold.

3 Cut a freezer paper template 5in x 3½in (12.7cm x 8.9cm). Centre the shiny side down on to wool felt and cut 7¼in x 5¾in (18.4cm x 14.6cm). Allowing 1⅛in (2.8cm) on every side, mark a line for cutting out the centre against the freezer paper edge. Cut out the centre.

4 Use a glue stick to stick the embroidered wool felt frame on the card stock paper, allowing an ⅛in (3mm) overhang of wool felt all sides. It's easier to put the felt frame face down and place the paper on top.

5 Cut gold or silver netting 9in (22.9cm) wide. With the back of the project facing, topstitch the netting to the frame through the paper and felt. Lay the netting across the back of the frame having just 1in (2.5cm) extending on both sides of the width of the frame. As you topstitch, feed the tucks of the netting into the stitches. Cut excess netting length at the end of the stitching. Turn the frame and lay the netting on to the opposite side and topstitch. Turn the frame and repeat with a length of netting for the frame length (there will be more overhang here). Trim the netting to 1in (2.5cm) on every side.

> ›› TIP
> *The invitation centre for text is 5in x 3½in (12.7cm x 8.9cm). You could print your party details before anchoring the embroidered wool felt piece.*

6 Using the template provided trace two flowers on to the dull side of some freezer paper. Press the shiny side of the freezer paper down on to wool felt, in the white, off-white, gold and silver colours. Cutting two of each will allow you to choose pleasing combinations.

7 Cut ribbon 12in (30.5cm) long for each flower. Create a double figure-of-eight and anchor with a threaded needle. Place two colours of wool felt flowers on top, bring the needle up through the flowers and then through a button. Bring the needle down through all layers and into one corner of the invitation. Repeat for extra strength through all layers and then knot. To finish, write the date, time and place on the invitation front.

Glitzy Decorations

These pretty decorations would be ideal to glam up a party at Christmas or New Year. Ribbon ties allow them to be used as tree decorations or to adorn a party table. There are seven designs, each with different embroidery designs.

You will need...

For seven decorations

- Off-white iridescent fabric ¼yd (0.25m) (width of fabric)
- Medium weight fusible interfacing ¼yd (0.25m)
- Wool felt in white, off-white, gold and grey (silver) 6in (15.2cm) square of each
- Netting in gold and silver ½yd (0.5m) of 54in/137cm wide of each
- Freezer paper
- Ribbon in gold and silver ⅛in (3mm) wide x 3yd (2¾m)
- Seven off-white buttons ⅜in (1cm) diameter
- DMC stranded cotton (floss): 645 grey, 648 light grey and 832 gold

Finished size:
4in (10.2cm) square

» Directions

1 See the Template section for the relevant templates. Trace seven 4in (10.2cm) squares on to the off-white fabric. Trace the embroidery designs on to the centre of the squares.

2 Back the seven squares with medium-weight interfacing following the manufacturer's instructions. I left my squares on one sheet of fabric until I had finished the embroidery. Work the embroidery as described in the panels at the end of the project.

3 Cut out the embroidered squares if necessary. Cut seven more squares from left-over off-white fabric for backings.

4 Cut two lengths of ribbon 8in (20.3cm) for each decoration. Pin in place where shown by the two Xs on the stocking template. Let the end of the ribbon extend slightly past the raw edge.

» TIP

When using a very narrow ribbon width I let the ribbon extend past the raw edge of fabric for extra strength, as ribbon can fray if cut too short. When trimming the fabric, I do not cut the ribbon ends but leave them long.

5 For all decorations, sew a backing to the front all around (right sides together), being careful not to catch the ribbon ends. Clip across the corners, turn through and press. Note: some gold and silver 'shimmer' ribbon can melt so be careful not to touch with a warm iron. Slipstitch the openings closed.

6 Cut strips of netting 5in (12.7cm) wide. With the back of the decoration facing you, place a doubled length of netting, 5in x 27in (12.7cm x 68.6cm), against the back of the decoration with ¾in (2cm) of netting extending on both sides. Topstitch the netting to the square, pushing the tucks of the netting into the stitches. When you reach the end, trim the netting. Turn the decoration and lay the netting on the opposite side down and topstitch in place. Repeat for the top and bottom, making sure the ribbon along the top is free of stitches. If the netting shifts while sewing move it back in place. Trim the netting ½in (1.3cm) from all sides of the square.

7 Trace two flowers on to the paper side of the freezer paper. Press the shiny side down and cut out as many flowers as you can from wool felts.

» TIP

When ribbon is used as a hanger, I have both long ends extend to the centre bottom of the decoration and then pin the backing, right sides together, with the ribbon sticking out. I start my seam at the bottom where the ribbon sticks out (leaving the ribbon free), sewing all around, pivoting at corners to the bottom edge again and stop my seam before I get to the ribbon. This is about a 1½in (3.8cm) gap. This way, I don't catch the ribbon in the seam. The ribbon also helps in turning my square, as when I pull the ribbon it brings the top to the opening where I can get a hold and pull through.

8 Cut seven pieces of ribbon each 12in (30.5cm). Create a double figure-of-eight and with a threaded needle anchor at the centre. Don't cut the thread yet. Choose two flower colours of wool felt. Lay the flowers on top of the ribbon, bring the needle up through both flowers and through one hole of a button. Place the cluster on the decoration and bring the needle back down through the button and all layers. Repeat up and through once more and then knot and cut the thread. Finish by tying the ribbon hanger together into a bow.

›› Embroidery

- Using a wash-away marker, mark lines for the embroidery. All embroidery is worked with two strands of embroidery cotton, unless otherwise stated.
- Stocking: stitch the cuff in light grey backstitch for the outside, straight stitches for the vertical lines and a lazy daisy stitch for the hanger. Work the stocking, heel and toe in gold backstitch. Work the lines in gold running stitch and the little stars in straight stitch. Add light grey French knot dots on the running stitch lines. **(1)**
- Santa: backstitch the ball on the hat, the hat trim, beard and moustache in light grey. Straight stitch the lines on the trim and the little stars on the beard in light grey. Backstitch the hat in gold with French knot dots. Work the eyes in grey French knots. **(2)**
- Snowman: backstitch the body and snow in light grey. Work the eyes, mouth and buttons in grey French knots. Backstitch the nose, scarf and arms in gold. Backstitch the trees in gold and the little stars in gold straight stitches. **(3)** (Continue in next panel.)

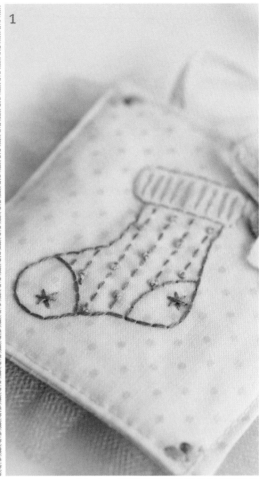

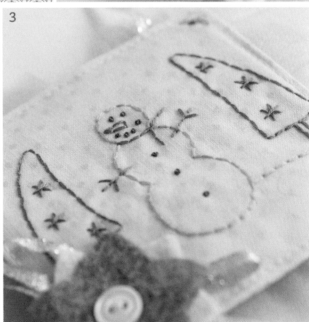

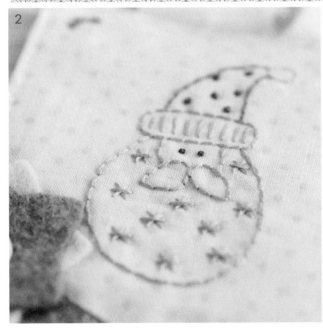

• House: backstitch the house, door and roof in gold. Work the door knob as a gold French knot. Backstitch the chimney, windows, snow and trees in light grey. Straight stitch the stars in light grey. **(4)**

• Presents: backstitch the outside of all packages and ribbons in gold. Work bows in gold lazy daisy stitches. Backstitch the diagonal stripes in light grey. Work the dots on two presents in light grey French knots and the stars on one present in light grey straight stitches. **(5)**

• Decorations: backstitch the pine bough scallop and all decoration shapes in gold. Straight stitch the needles on the bough and the star on the centre decoration in gold. Backstitch all decoration tops and hangers in light grey. Work the dots on the left and right decorations and the bough berries in light grey French knots. Work the dot at the base of the centre decoration as a gold French knot. **(6)**

• Reindeer: backstitch the head, antlers, body and legs in gold. Work the ears and tail as gold lazy daisy stitches. Work the nose as a gold French knot and the eyes as grey French knots. Straight stitch the stars in light grey. **(7)**

• Corner details on all decorations: use three strands of thread for all dots. Use two strands for lazy daisy stitches. Alternate colours for the corner detail – work some gold dots with light grey lazy daisy stitches and some silver dots with gold lazy daisy stitches.

Christmas Garland

Remember those paper chain garlands most of us made as children? Well this project takes that idea to a new level in pretty, shimmering fabrics. The instructions are for a 1yd (1m) length.

You will need...

For 12 rings

- Off-white iridescent fabric ⅓yd (0.3m) of 45in (114.3cm) wide or ½yd (0.5m) of 43in (109cm) wide)

- Medium-weight fusible interfacing ¾yd (0.75m)

- Netting in gold and silver 1¼yd (1.25m) of 54in (137cm) wide of each

- Wool felt in yellow (gold), grey (silver), white and off-white 9in (22.9cm) square of each

- Freezer paper

- Ribbon in gold and silver ⅛in (3mm) wide x 2yd (2m) of each

- Twenty-four off-white buttons ⅜in (1cm) diameter

- DMC stranded cotton (floss): 648 light grey and 832 gold

Finished size of garland:
One ring is approximately 3¼in–4in (8.2cm–10.2cm), so twelve rings are 36in (91.4cm) when draped

» Directions

1. See the Template section for the relevant templates. With a wash-away pen or pencil, draw twelve strips 2in x 11in (5cm x 27.9cm) on to the right side of the off-white fabric. Trace the design on to each strip as on the template. Draw four each of the three designs. Cut twelve from excess fabric 2in x 11in (5cm x 27.9cm) for ring backings. Back the fabric strips with medium-weight interfacing. Work the embroidery as described in the panel.

2. After the embroidery is finished, cut out the strips along the lines you have drawn 2in x 11in (5cm x 27.9cm). With right sides together, sew a backing strip to the embroidered strip, leaving an opening for turning. Clip the corners, turn through and press the strips. The opening will be closed by topstitching in the next step.

>> Embroidery

- Work French knots with three strands of gold or light grey. Work running stitches with two strands of gold or light grey. **(1)**
- Work lazy daisy stitches with two strands of gold or light grey. **(2)**
- Work stars with two strands of gold or light grey. **(3)**
- Alternate colours in the patterns as shown in the photographs. For instance, on two of the strips I worked gold French knots with light grey running stitches between. For the other two I worked light grey French knots with gold running stitches between. Alternate for the other designs as well.

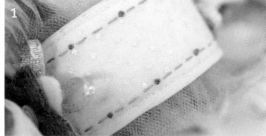

3 Cut netting strips 3in (7.6cm) wide, cutting six from silver and six from gold. Fold each in half so the netting is 3in x 27in (7.6cm x 68.6cm). With the back of the strip facing you, start with one end of the netting at the top of the strip and extending ¾in (2cm) from both edges. As you topstitch the netting, feed the tucks into the stitches. Cut off excess at the end. If you see you may not have enough at the end, add another doubled strip. If the netting slides to one edge more than the other, adjust back to the correct distance from each side. Topstitch the other side, laying the tucks down with your hand as you feed. Trim the netting to ½in (1.3cm) from the sides of the strip.

4 For the wool felt flowers, trace four or five flowers on to the paper side of some freezer paper. Press the shiny side of the freezer paper on to felt and cut out as many as you can on your 9in (22.9cm) square. Peel off and repeat with every colour. These will give you plenty of colour combinations to play with.

5 Cut twelve lengths from the gold and silver ribbons, each 12in (30.5cm) long. Take each length and make a double figure-of-eight shape. Using a needle and knotted thread, anchor in the middle with a couple of stitches through all layers. Cut the thread leaving a ½in (1.3cm) tail – there is no need to knot.

6 Pin the garland rings in alternating silver or gold netting edges, with a ½in (1.3cm) overlap on each ring. For each ring choose a ribbon figure-of-eight, two flowers and a button. The rings are decorated and joined together simultaneously, as follows. Thread a needle with a knotted doubled thread. Bring the needle up through the ribbon figure-of-eight, through two colours of flowers and through one hole of a button placed over an overlap of two rings. Bring the needle down through the button and through all layers. Bring the needle back up again and through twice more for strength. Knot the thread and cut on the inside of the ring. Remove the pin. Repeat the process for the opposite side of the ring but bring the needle and thread through just once to hold in place.

Basic Techniques

This section describes the basic techniques and stitches you will need to make the projects in the book.

Using this Book

- The projects in this book were made using imperial inches. Metric conversions are given in brackets but use *either* imperial *or* metric, as the systems are not interchangeable. The best results will be obtained using inches.
- All seams are sewn with a ¼ in (6mm) seam allowance, unless stated otherwise. Cutting instructions include a ¼ in (6mm) seam allowance.
- Appliqué design pieces are finished sizes. The appliqué templates do not include a ¼ in (6mm) allowance for turning under. If you choose to turn under your appliqué designs, add ¼ in (6mm) around the edges.
- The thicker lines in the templates are appliqué, while the thinner lines are embroidery.

Tracing Templates and Designs

Trace designs by centring them over a light source. This may be a light box or even a sunny window. Place your paper design to be traced first, then your fabric piece over this. It helps to tape your design in place so you can take a rest and come back to it if needed.

You can also trace the templates on to freezer paper and iron the paper on to fabric before cutting out – see Using Wool Felt for Appliqué. While it is more time consuming, it is precise. You can use the freezer paper many times.

Use your favourite tracing tool to trace designs on to fabric. Mine is a blue wash-away pen but you may prefer tailor's chalk, pencil or pen.

Backing with Wadding (Batting)

I like to make my quilt tops and have them traced and ready for the embroidery work. Then I back my tops with a lightweight quilt wadding to create a 'quilted' effect while working the embroidery. Cut the wadding larger than the quilt top, trimming it after all quilting is finished. You can hold the backing in place by pinning, tacking (basting) or with fabric spray adhesive. This method gives stability while stitching, allows the threads to carry over from point to point without the thread being seen from the front and, most importantly, plumps up the stitches so that they have body and are not flat.

Using Embroidery Threads

I have used DMC stranded embroidery cotton (floss) for the projects in this book. These threads are widely available in a vast array of colours. In the embroidery sections of each project, I have indicated colours to use, but you can, of course, change these as you like.

Embroidery threads are usually formed from six strands and can be split into single strands. The number of strands to use for each piece of work (one, two or three) is indicated in the instructions for each project.

Using Fusible Products

I have used fusible web and fusible interfacing (including craft-weight interfacing) for the projects. You can buy it by the yard/metre or in pre-cut sheets. Always read the manufacturer's instructions before use.

DOUBLE-SIDED FUSIBLE WEB

This is often sold as Bondaweb or Wonderweb and can be used as a quick method of attaching an appliqué piece to a background fabric. One side looks like paper and you can trace the shape you want on to it (the shape will come out in reverse). Cut around roughly and iron it on to the back of the felt or fabric you want to appliqué. Cut carefully on the traced lines, peel off the paper backing and iron on to the background fabric to fuse. If using this method for wool felt appliqué, you can omit the whipstitch edging and move straight to the embroidery.

FREEZER PAPER

Freezer paper is available by the yard/metre or in pre-cut sheets. It has a shiny, plastic-coated side that will stick to fabric when ironed, so it is very useful for appliqué. It is thin enough to allow designs to be traced on to the dull side of the paper and be cut out, and can be removed and reapplied several times.

FUSIBLE INTERFACING

I use single-sided interfacing on some flimsy fabrics to give them more body.

Using Wool Felt for Appliqué

Always pre-rinse wool felts prior to use. Run under warm water in the sink, rinsing until the water runs almost clear. Squeeze out excess water and allow to air dry before ironing. This will ensure that dyes are removed and that the wool is shrunk to size. It is good to get into the habit of rinsing felt as soon as you buy it.

Use freezer paper to cut your wool felt design pieces. Trace the appliqué design on to the dull side of the freezer paper (there are no seams to turn under with wool-felt appliqué). With a dry iron, iron the shiny side of the paper on to the wool felt and it will stick temporarily. Cut out on traced lines and peel the paper from the felt. You can use a freezer paper template many times.

Glue your wool felt appliqué pieces to your project – they only need the tiniest spots of glue to hold. This is a method I use with all appliqué. If you haven't done this in the past, you will love the fact that there are no pins to lose or catch threads. After gluing, I press all my pieces briefly with the iron. This anchors them and also makes the surface a little flatter and neater to whipstitch. Using one strand of embroidery thread matching the colour of the wool felt, I use a simple whipstitch to sew to the background for a very neat look.

I use a blue wash-away pen to mark embroidery lines on wool felt. After stitching, I remove these lines with a damp sponge, blotting sparingly. Chalk also works well with wool felt and marks can simply be brushed away. Wool felt does not trace very well so I hope you become confident enough to apply the simple embroidery lines freehand. You will get very good at doing French knot dots and lazy daisy leaves on your own!

Binding a Quilt or Cushion

1 Cut lengths of binding fabric to a width of 2½in (6.3cm). Join strips together to create sufficient length to go all round plus a few inches extra for corners and ends. Fold the left-hand edge of the strip up to form a diagonal edge and press the binding strip in half across wrong sides together along the whole length (see Fig1A).

2 Pin the raw edge of the binding strip in place against the raw edge of the right side of the quilt, with the fold pointing inwards, 1in (2.5cm) or so away from the corner. Leaving the 1in (2.5cm) (the tail) free, sew a ¼in (6mm) seam all the way along, stopping ¼in (6mm) from the next corner (Fig 1B).

3 Fold the binding up from the corner to a 45-degree angle, keeping the raw edges aligned (Fig 1C).

4 Fold the binding back down again to line up with the right-hand edge of the quilt (Fig 1D). Reverse stitch over the edge and continue sewing to within ¼in (6mm) of the next corner, then turn as you did before. When you reach the starting point, tuck the end into the folded tail and stitch over. Trim the wadding (batting) and backing even with the raw edge of the binding and quilt. Trim corners on the diagonal to ease the fold of the mitred corner.

5 Fold the binding over to the back of the quilt and stitch in place, folding the binding at each corner to form a neat mitre as shown Fig 1E.

Fig 1A

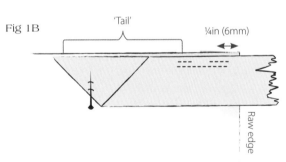

Fig 1B

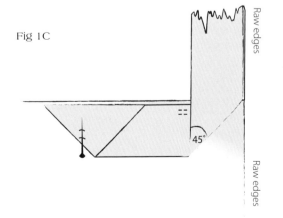

Fig 1C

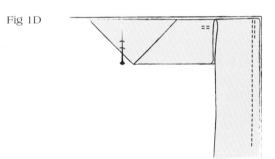

Fig 1D

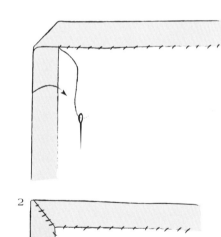

Fig 1E

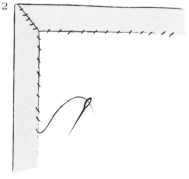

Working the Stitches

BACKSTITCH

Bring the needle up to the front of the fabric. Moving backwards, take the needle down ⅛in (3mm) from the original hole. Bring the needle back up ⅛in (3mm) ahead of the original hole. Bring the needle back down into the original hole. Repeat, bringing the needle back up ahead of the last hole.

FRENCH KNOT

Bring the needle up to the top. Wrap the thread around the needle one, two or three times depending on the desired size of the knot. Put the needle back into the original hole, being careful not to let the loops unwrap. Pull the needle from the back, slowly drawing the thread through all the loops, creating a knot on the front.

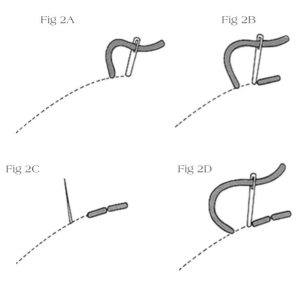

Fig 2A   Fig 2B

Fig 2C   Fig 2D

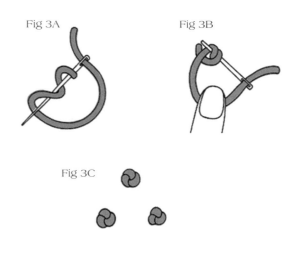

Fig 3A   Fig 3B

Fig 3C

LAZY DAISY STITCH

Bring the needle up to the top at the base of the stitch point (think of a teardrop – the base is the point, the round part is the loop). Bring the needle back down to the base in the same hole without pulling the thread all the way through. Let the thread make a loop and bring the needle back up to the top of the loop at the required distance from the base. Catch the loop with your needle and pull until the thread loop is the shape of a teardrop. Bridge the loop with a small stitch to anchor it in place.

RUNNING STITCH

A quilting stitch is a running stitch. Bring the needle up to the top. Make a stitch at the required distance (usually ⅛in/3mm) bringing the needle down. Bring the needle back up, again leaving a distance in between. Repeat until the design is complete.

Fig 5

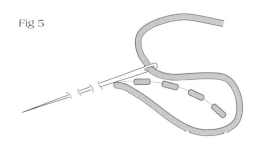

Fig 4A

Fig 4B

SATIN STITCH

Bring the needle up to the top of the shape you want to fill in. Bring the needle back down across the shape to the bottom. Bring the next stitch up right next to the first stitch, and then down, right next to the previous second stitch. Fill in with stitches snug against each other LIKE THIS until the entire space is filled.

Fig 6A   Fig 6B

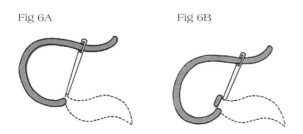

SLIPSTITCH

This stitch is used to close openings. Bring the needle to the front of one side a scant 1/16in (1.5mm). Catch the other side with a scant 1/16in (1.5mm) stitch. Draw up the thread bringing these two sides together. Bring the needle back to the original side and repeat, moving across the opening until it is closed.

Fig 7

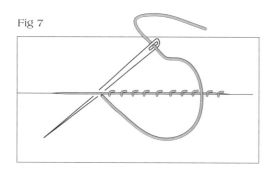

TOPSTITCH

This is usually done with a sewing machine. Using a 1/8in (3mm) to 1/4in (6mm) straight stitch, sew through all layers, anchoring your pieces to the backing fabric.

Fig 8

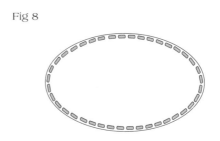

WHIPSTITCH

This stitch is used to anchor appliqué pieces to backing fabric. Bring the needle up 1/8in (3mm) into the appliqué. Move the needle horizontally 1/8in (3mm) and down into the backing fabric. On the wrong side, move the needle diagonally and forward 1/8in (3mm) up again into the appliqué piece and again 1/8in (3mm) down into the backing fabric. Repeat all around.

Fig 9

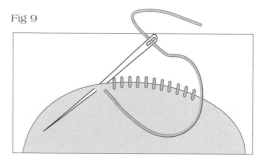

Templates

Important note: *most of the templates have been reduced to fit the page so before using you will need to enlarge them on a photocopier by the percentage given. See also Tracing Templates and Designs in Basic Techniques.*

Vintage Christmas chapter
Tinsel Tree Scrapbook
Template – shown half size so enlarge by 200%

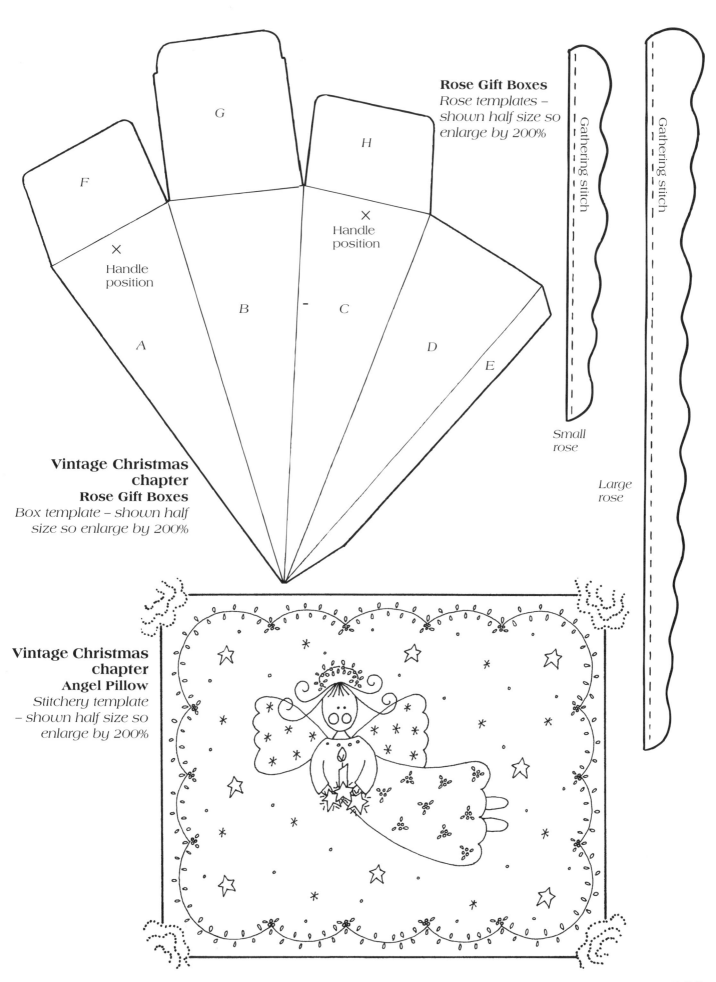

Rose Gift Boxes
*Rose templates –
shown half size so
enlarge by 200%*

F

G

H

✕
Handle
position

✕
Handle
position

A

B

C

D

E

Gathering stitch

Gathering stitch

*Small
rose*

*Large
rose*

**Vintage Christmas
chapter
Rose Gift Boxes**
*Box template – shown half
size so enlarge by 200%*

**Vintage Christmas
chapter
Angel Pillow**
*Stitchery template
– shown half size so
enlarge by 200%*

Celebration Table chapter
Celebration Wine Scarves
Templates – shown half size so enlarge by 200%

Celebration Table chapter
Christmas Table Runner
Motif templates – shown half size so enlarge by 200%

Celebration Table chapter
Festive Napkin Wraps
Templates – shown half size so enlarge by 200%
Dashed lines indicate where appliqué pieces overlap

Celebration Table chapter
Christmas Table Runner
Ttemplate 1 – shown half size
so enlarge by 200%

Dashed lines on the motif
templates indicate where some
pieces overlap
Thinner lines indicate embroidery

Solid line indicates blue
background
Dashed outer line indicates
dark blue backing

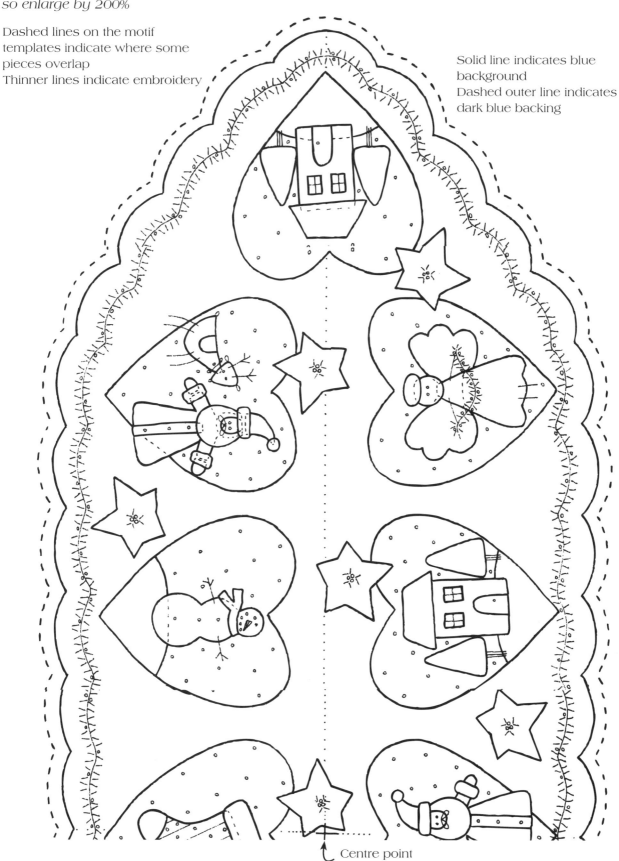

Centre point

Centre point

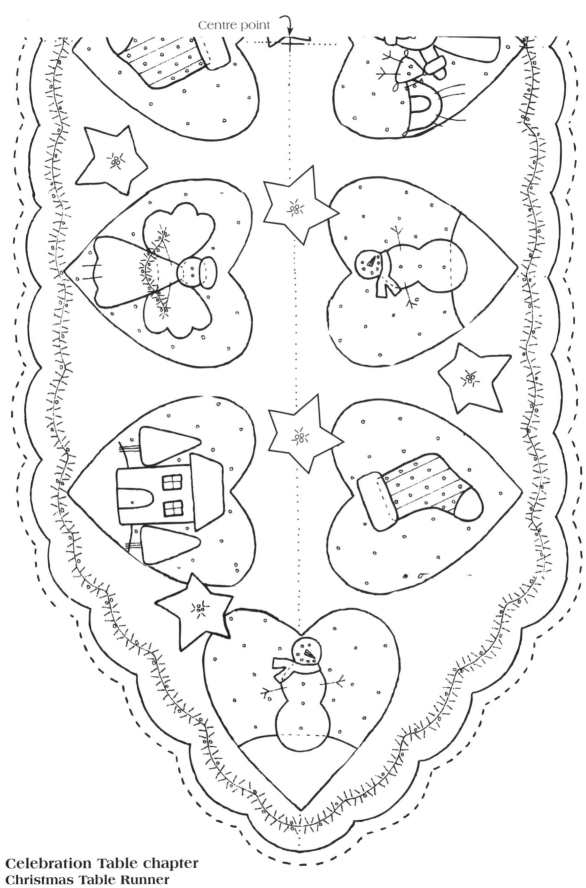

Celebration Table chapter
Christmas Table Runner
Template 2 – shown half size so enlarge by 200%

Christmas Kids chapter
Fun Finger Puppets
Templates – shown full size

Dashed lines indicate where appliqué parts overlap

Reindeer back cut 1

Reindeer head cut 1

Sleeve piece

Sewing line

Fold line

Antler cut 2

Nose cut 1

Ear cut 2

Reindeer body cut 1

Hoof cut 2

Arm cut 2

Cheek cut 2

Head cut 1 from brown and 1 from peach

Angel wing cut 1

Hair cut

Dress cut 2

Halo cut 1

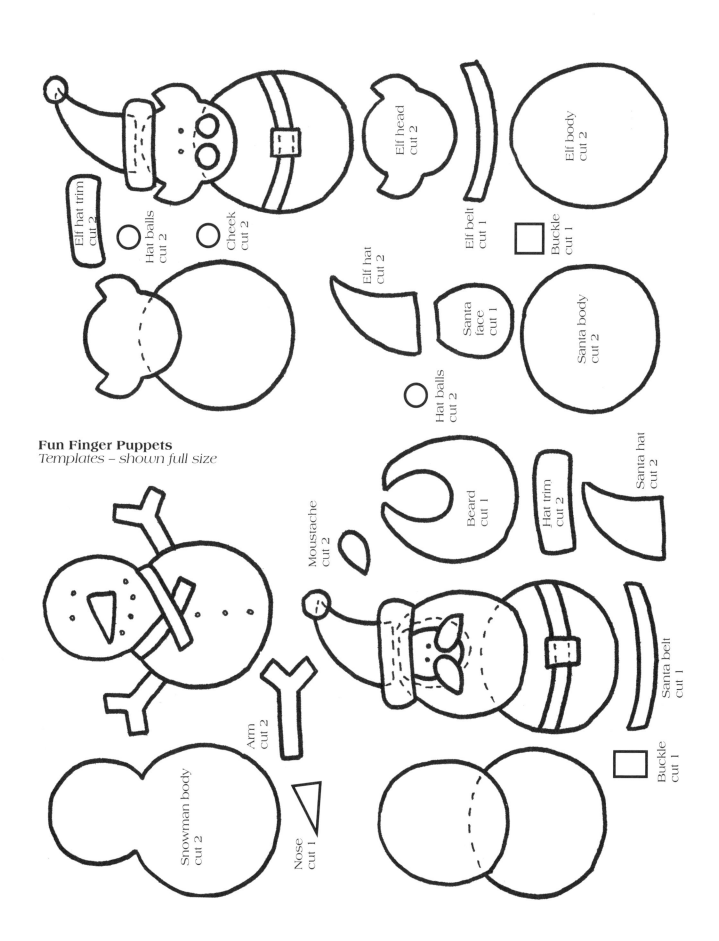

Fun Finger Puppets
Templates – shown full size

Elf hat trim
cut 2

Hat balls
cut 2

Cheek
cut 2

Elf head
cut 2

Elf belt
cut 1

Buckle
cut 1

Elf body
cut 2

Elf hat
cut 2

Santa face
cut 1

Santa body
cut 2

Hat balls
cut 2

Santa hat
cut 2

Moustache
cut 2

Beard
cut 1

Hat trim
cut 2

Arm
cut 2

Santa belt
cut 1

Snowman body
cut 2

Nose
cut 1

Buckle
cut 1

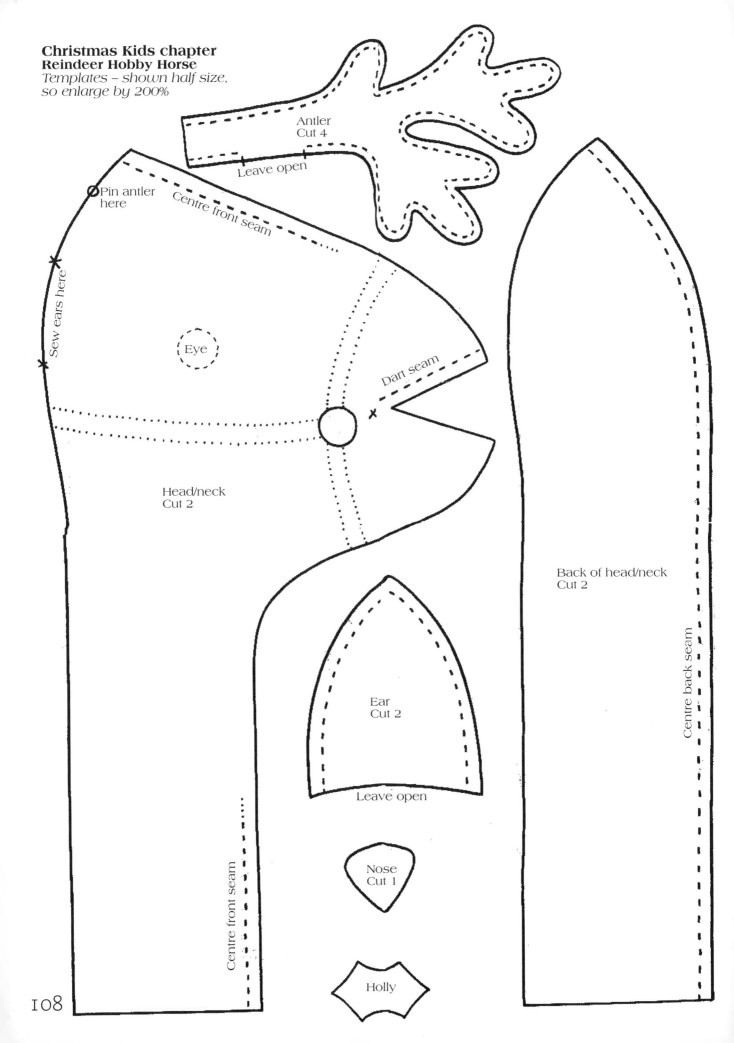

Christmas Kids chapter
Reindeer Hobby Horse
Templates – shown half size,
so enlarge by 200%

Antler
Cut 4

Leave open

Pin antler
here

Centre front seam

Sew ears here

Eye

Dart seam

Head/neck
Cut 2

Back of head/neck
Cut 2

Ear
Cut 2

Leave open

Centre back seam

Centre front seam

Nose
Cut 1

Holly

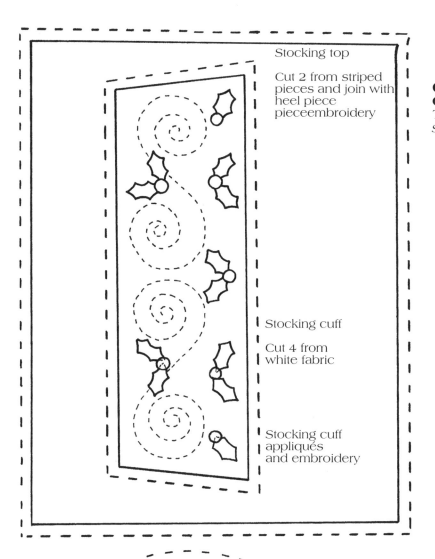

Stocking top

Cut 2 from striped pieces and join with heel piece pieceembroidery

Christmas Kids chapter
Christmas Stocking
Templates – shown half size,
so enlarge by 200%

Stocking cuff

Cut 4 from white fabric

Stocking cuff appliqués and embroidery

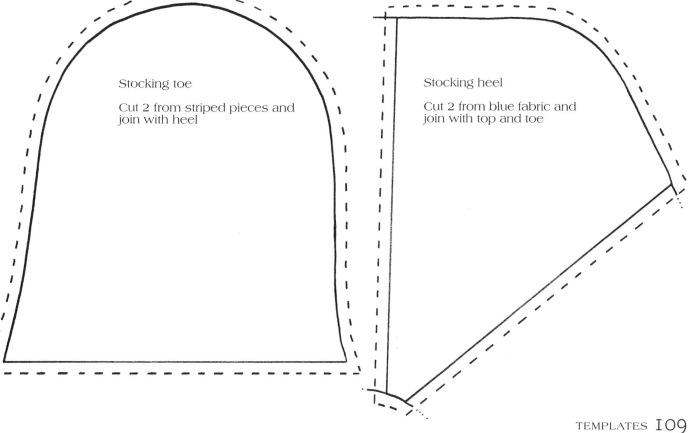

Stocking toe

Cut 2 from striped pieces and join with heel

Stocking heel

Cut 2 from blue fabric and join with top and toe

Christmas Kids chapter
Christmas Stocking
*Appliqué and Embroidery
Templates – shown half size
so enlarge by 200%*

Dashed lines indicate where
appliqué pieces overlap
Spiral dashed lines indicate
surface embroidery

Cuff

White Christmas chapter
Snowflake Ornaments
Templates – shown half size so enlarge by 200%

One quarter of the circle – trace one quarter and then flip to create the next quarter. Copy both quarters to create the other half of the circle

Ornament 1
One quarter of
an 11in (27.9cm)
diameter circle

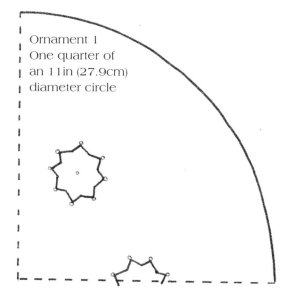

Ornament 2
One quarter of
an 11in (27.9cm)
diameter circle

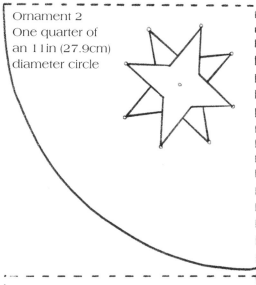

Ornament 3
One quarter of
an 11in (27.9cm)
diameter circle

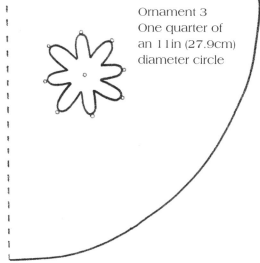

White Christmas chapter
Sparkly Candle Mats
Templates – shown half size so enlarge by 200%

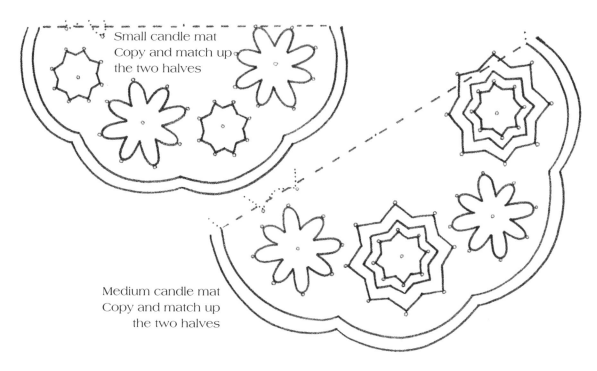

Small candle mat
Copy and match up
the two halves

Medium candle mat
Copy and match up
the two halves

White Christmas chapter
Large Candle Mat
Template – shown half size so enlarge by 200%

White Christmas chapter
Tree Skirt

Template (one sixth of the design) – shown quarter size, so enlarge by 400%

Snowflake at the edge of the design part shown – enlarge by the same percentage as the main segment

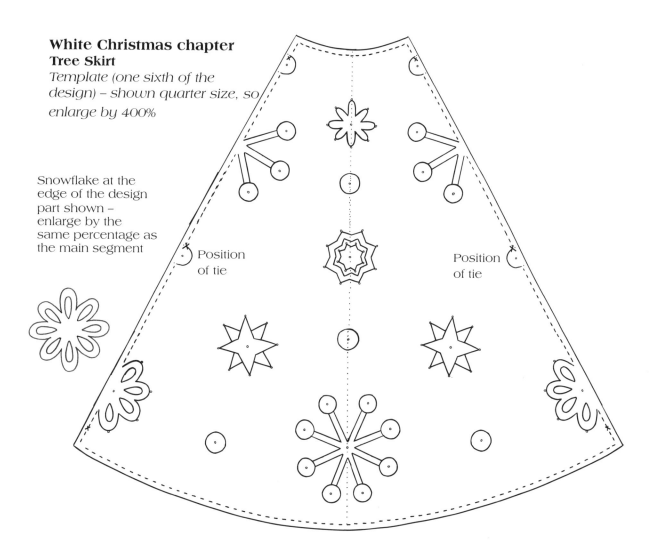

Position of tie

Position of tie

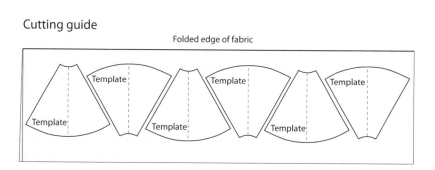

Cutting guide

Folded edge of fabric

Template
Template
Template
Template
Template
Template

Sew six pieces together for the front of the skirt and the same for the back of the skirt

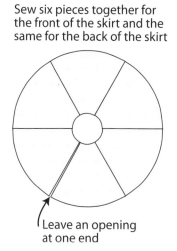

Leave an opening at one end

Seasonal Kitchen chapter
Sweet Gift Tags
Templates – shown full size

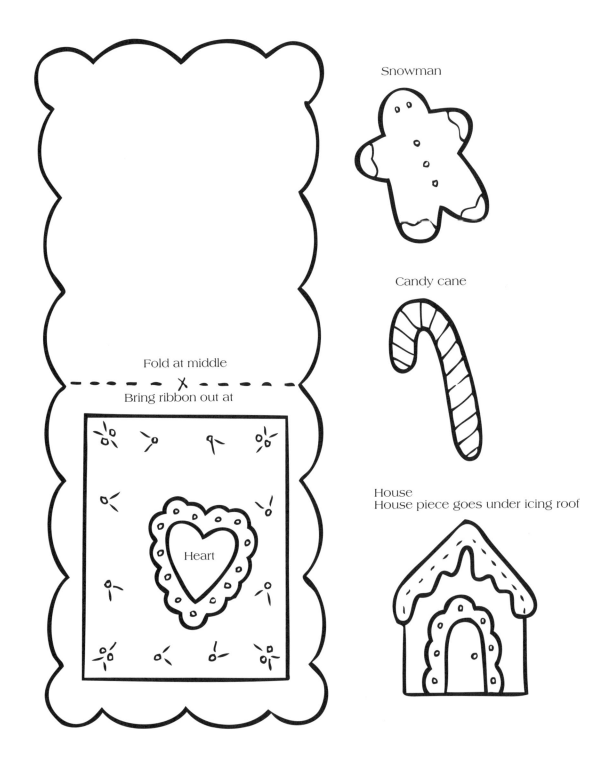

Snowman

Candy cane

Fold at middle

Bring ribbon out at

Heart

House
House piece goes under icing roof

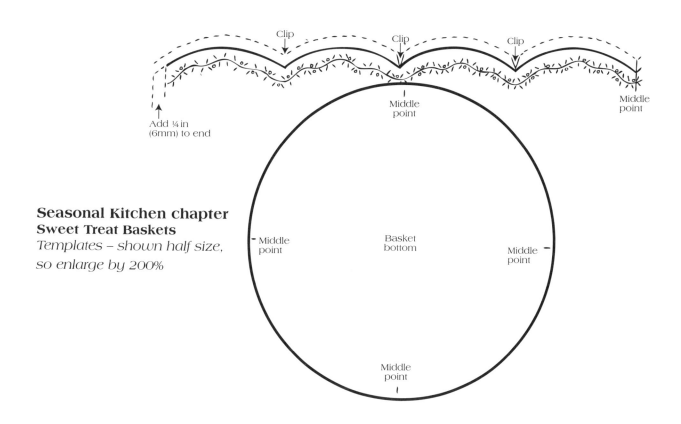

Clip

Clip

Clip

Middle
point

Middle
point

Add ¼ in
(6mm) to end

Seasonal Kitchen chapter
Sweet Treat Baskets
Templates – shown half size,
so enlarge by 200%

Middle
point

Basket
bottom

Middle
point

Middle
point

Ric-rac embroidery

Seasonal Kitchen chapter
Sweet Treat Basket and
Gingerbread Apron
Templates – shown half size,
so enlarge by 200%

Roof top

Cupcake base

Cupcake top

Gingerbread
house appliqué
pieces

Third roof piece

Window

Second roof piece

Roof side

First roof piece

Window
scallop

Icing

Door scallop

House

Door

Candy
cane

Seasonal Kitchen chapter
Gingerbread Apron
Templates – shown full size

Gingerbread pocket

Solid line = sewing line

Dashed line = cutting line

House pocket

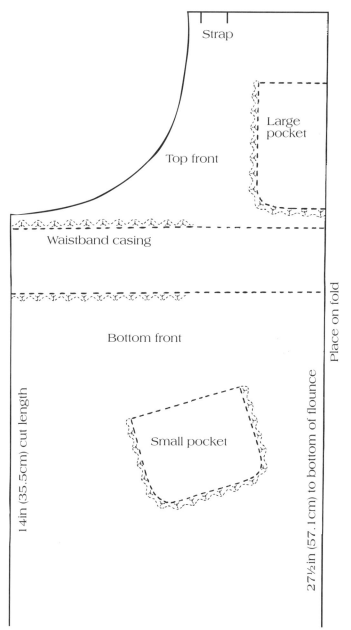

Strap

Top front

Large
pocket

Waistband casing

Bottom front

Small pocket

14in (35.5cm) cut length

27½in (57.1cm) to bottom of flounce

Place on fold

Seasonal Kitchen chapter
Gingerbread Apron
*Templates top front, waistband and
bottom front – shown quarter size
so enlarge by 400%*

Add ½in (1.3cm) for seams

Place on fold

12in (30.5cm)

Seasonal Kitchen chapter
Gingerbread Apron
*Template bottom flounce – shown
half size so enlarge by 200%*

Position of candy
cane appliqués

12in (30.5cm)

Christmas Night chapter
Christmas Stocking
Template – shown half size so
enlarge by 200%

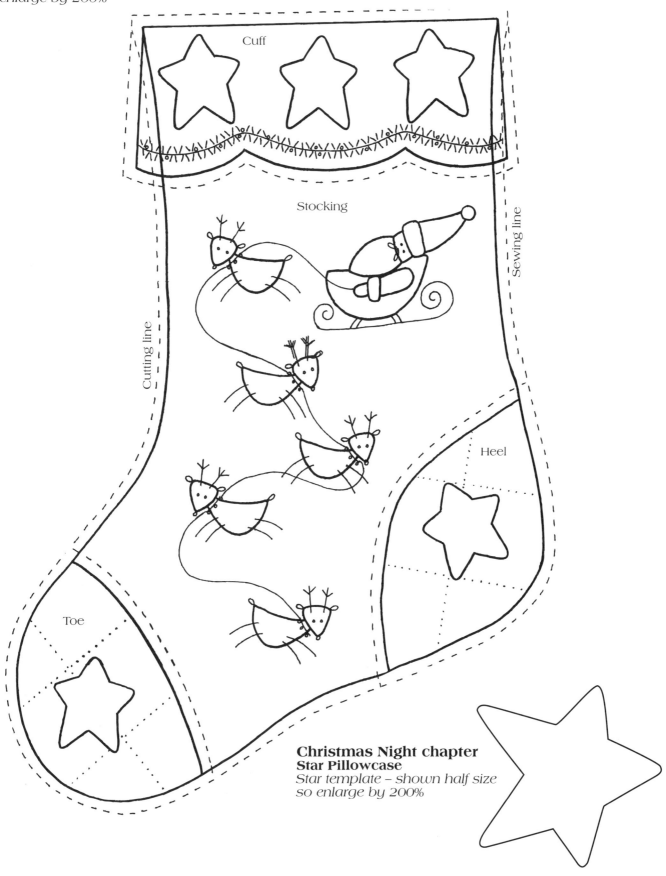

Cuff

Stocking

Sewing line

Cutting line

Heel

Toe

Christmas Night chapter
Star Pillowcase
Star template – shown half size
so enlarge by 200%

Christmas Night chapter
Christmas Night Quilt

Fireplace Block template – shown at 45%, so enlarge by 222.2%

The inner border is also included on this block to show the embroidery placement, so use this design on the other blocks too

Thick lines on the templates indicate appliqué and thin lines indicate embroidery

A dashed line indicates where appliqué pieces overlap

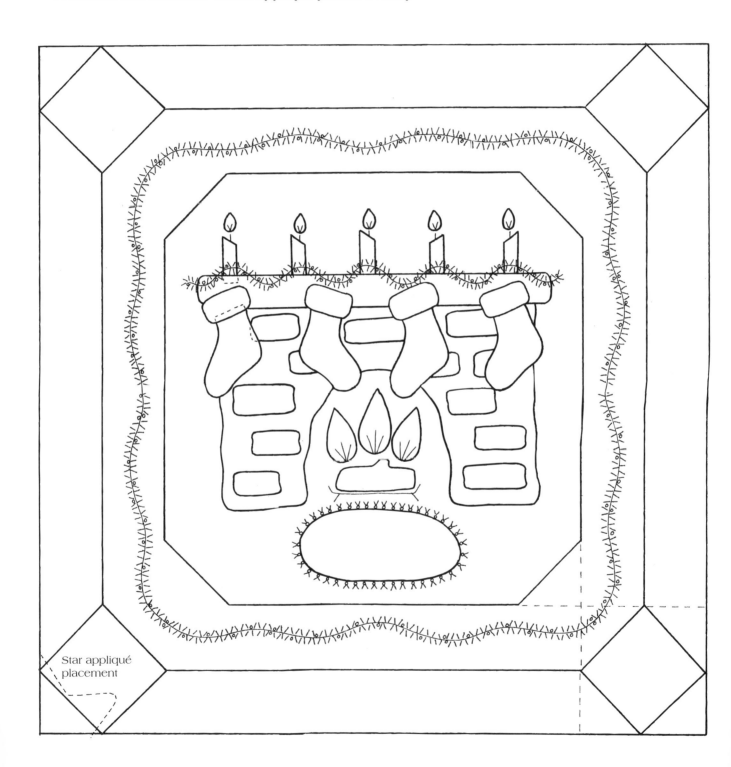

Star appliqué placement

Christmas Night Quilt

Snowman Block template – shown at 45%, so enlarge by 222.2%

Mark the embroidery on the inner border as shown in the Fireplace Block

Christmas Night Quilt

Ornament Block template – shown at 45%, so enlarge by 222.2%

Mark the embroidery on the inner border as shown in the Fireplace Block

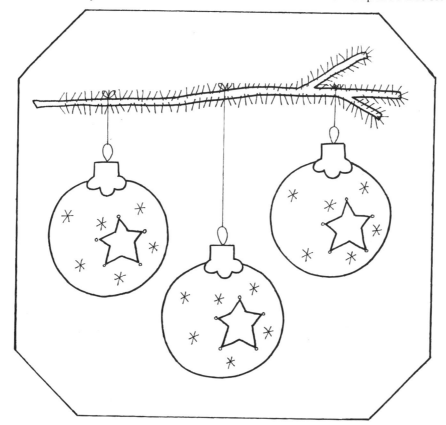

Christmas Night Quilt

Ornament Block template – shown at 45% so enlarge by 222.2%

Mark the embroidery on the inner border as shown in the Fireplace Block

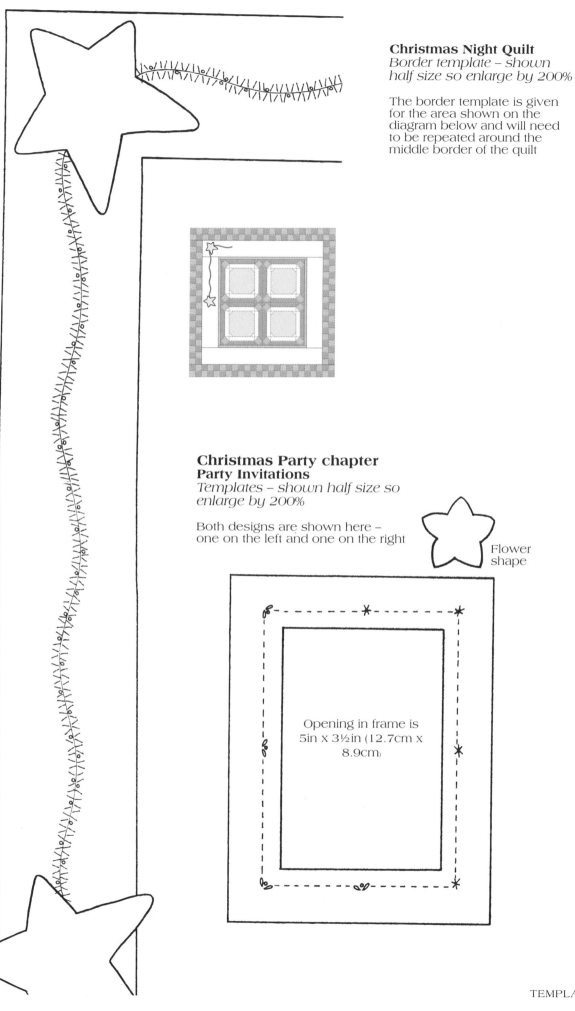

Christmas Night Quilt
Border template – shown half size so enlarge by 200%

The border template is given for the area shown on the diagram below and will need to be repeated around the middle border of the quilt

Christmas Party chapter
Party Invitations
Templates – shown half size so enlarge by 200%

Both designs are shown here – one on the left and one on the right

Flower shape

Opening in frame is 5in x 3½in (12.7cm x 8.9cm)

Christmas Party chapter
Glitzy Decorations
Templates – shown half size so enlarge by 200%

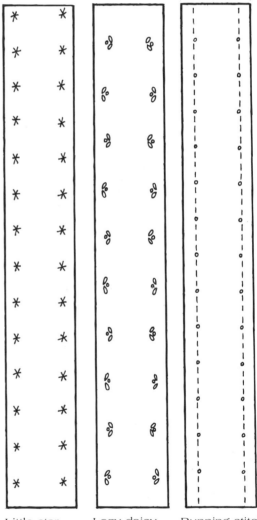

Flower shape for decorations

Christmas Party chapter
Christmas Garland
Templates – shown half size so enlarge by 200%

Each design shows the finished size of 1½in x 10½in (3.8cm x 26.7cm)

Flower shape for garland

Little star design

Lazy daisy design

Running stitch and French knot design

SUPPLIERS

U.K. Suppliers

RUCRAFT

www.rucraft.co.uk

For fabrics and haberdashery

– – – – – – – – – – – – – – – –

THE ETERNAL MAKER

89 Oving Road, Chichester, West Sussex
PO19 7EW

www.eternalmaker.com

For wool felt, haberdashery and craft fabrics

– – – – – – – – – – – – – – – –

JOHN LEWIS

Draycott Avenue, London SW3 2NA

www.johnlewis.com

For fabrics and haberdashery

– – – – – – – – – – – – – – – –

WHALEYS

Harris Court, Great Horton, Bradford BD7 4EQ

www.whaleys-bradford.ltd.uk

For fabrics, wadding (batting) and interfacing

– – – – – – – – – – – – – – – –

U.S. Suppliers

HILL CREEK DESIGNS

10159 Buena Vista Avenue, Santee, CA 92071

Tel: (619) 562 5799

www.hillcreekdesigns.com

For buttons

– – – – – – – – – – – – – – – –

HOMESPUN HEARTH

15954 Jackson Creek Pkwy, Suite B #546,
Monument, CO 80132

Tel: (866) 346 0414

www.homespunhearth.com

For online fabrics, wool felt and needlecraft
supplies

– – – – – – – – – – – – – – – –

SIERRA COTTONS & WOOLS

2301 N. Sierra Highway, Bishop, CA 93514

Tel: (760) 872-9209

www.sierracottonsandwools.com

Email: sierracottonsandwools@yahoo.com

For wools, wool felts, fabrics, floss, and kits

– – – – – – – – – – – – – – – –

WOOL FELT CENTRAL

P.O. Box 184, Cozad, NE 69130

Tel: (308) 784-2010

www.woolfeltcentral.com

Email: prariepointjunction@yahoo.com

For fabrics, wool felts and kits (US only)

– – – – – – – – – – – – – – – –

ABOUT THE AUTHOR

Barri Sue Gaudet has been around fabrics and crafts for most of her life. After many years of working in fabric and quilt shops, she began her own pattern company 'Bareroots' in 1999. She has enjoyed creating original designs of all kinds ever since. Barri Sue's designs include little quilts, cushions and stitcheries and are easily recognized by the delightful elements of nature and sweet little motifs contained in all. Along with the joy of her work involving what she loves, Barri Sue enjoys the opportunities to teach and meet others who love embroidery.
Barri Sue's other hobbies include knitting, painting, friends and being outdoors. After raising two sons, Barri Sue moved to a tiny mountain town in the California Sierra Nevada Mountains named June Lake. She lives there with her husband Ron, a dog and two old cats. She has recently opened a stitchery and knitting shop in Bishop, California called Sierra Cottons & Wools.

Acknowledgments:

Christmas is the time to remember all the wonderful people in your life and I would like to take the opportunity to thank those of you who had a special part in helping me create this book. For my co-workers at the shop, thank you for allowing me to be away and tucked into my sewing room for so many days. Margi, your spirit is like Christmas every day. Thank you for all your time and especially your enthusiasm. Sheri, thank you for your ideas and keen contributions to colour. Lesley, thank you for always understanding what we really do and for listening. To my 'oody' friends, thank you for your support and willingness to always give a hand.
And finally, a big thank you to the David & Charles (F&W Media International) staff of Sarah, Jeni, Linda and Mia, for your patience and experience in helping me create another beautiful book.

INDEX

A DAVID & CHARLES BOOK
© F&W Media International, Ltd 2012

David & Charles is an imprint of F&W Media International, Ltd
Brunel House, Forde Close, Newton Abbot, TQ12 4PU, UK

F&W Media International, Ltd is a subsidiary of F+W Media, Inc
10151 Carver Road, Suite #200, Blue Ash, OH 45242, USA

A catalogue record for this book is available from the British Library.

ISBN-13: 978-1-4463-0184-5 Paperback
ISBN-10: 1-4463-0184-2 Paperback

Printed in China by RR Donnelley for:
F&W Media International, Ltd
Brunel House, Forde Close, Newton Abbot, TQ12 4PU, UK

10 9 8 7 6 5 4 3 2 1

Acquisitions Editor: Sarah Callard
Desk Editor: Jeni Hennah
Project Editor: Linda Clements
Design Manager: Sarah Clark
Senior Designer: Mia Farrant
Photographers: Sian Irvine and Jack Kirby
Senior Production Controller: Kelly Smith

F+W Media publishes high quality books on a wide range of subjects.
For more great book ideas visit: www.rucraft.co.uk